OUTDOOR
STONEWORK

QUARRY

LAUREL SAVILLE

OUTDOOR
STONEWORK

THE TIMELESS, PRACTICAL, AND AESTHETIC VALUE OF STONE

BEVERLY MASSACHUSETTS

QUARRY BOOKS

First published in the United States of America by
Quarry Books, a member of
Quayside Publishing Group
100 Cummings Center
Suite 406-L
Beverly, Massachusetts 01915-6101
Telephone: (978) 282-9590
Fax: (978) 283-2742
www.quarrybooks.com

Library of Congress Cataloging-in-Publication Data
Saville, Laurel.
    Outdoor stonework / Laurel Saville.
        p. cm.
    ISBN 1-59253-321-3
    1. Garden structures. 2. Building, Stone. 3. Stonemasonry. I. Title.
    TH4961.S278 2008
    693'.1--dc22

                                                        2007032796
                                                        CIP

ISBN-13: 978-1-59253-321-3
ISBN-10: 1-59253-321-3

10 9 8 7 6 5 4 3 2

Cover and interior design: Sandra Salamony
Cover images, front cover: Clive Nichols Garden Photography/www.clivenichols.com, main image; Norm Plate, top, left; Linda Oyama Bryan/Craig Bergmann Landscape Design, top, middle; Courtesy of biota, A Landscape Design + Build Firm, top right.
Back cover: Brian Westbury/Hursthouse Landscape Architects & Contractors, left; Courtesy of Sam H. Williamson & Associates, second from left; Hans Matschukat, second from right; Hausman Photography, right.
Illustration: Melanie Powell
Editor: Laura B. Smith
Illustrations: Melanie Powell
Technical Editor: Philip Schmidt

Printed in China

CONTENTS

PART TWO:
STONEWORK PROJECTS

"*The finest workers in stone are not copper or steel tools, but the gentle touches of air and water working at their leisure with a liberal allowance of time.*"
—*Henry David Thoreau*

THE BEAUTY
AND ALLURE OF STONE

LITTLE BOYS THROW THEM. Wallers stack them. Water wears them. Artists shape them. Plants caress them. Animals make their homes among them. Early peoples sheltered within them and even painted murals on them.

We scale mountains and stand atop what the glaciers left behind of the scraped earth. We have an irresistible urge to pick up flattened stones and skip them across or simply toss them into bodies of water, watching in blind fascination as they interrupt the surface tension in echoing patterns. We pile them into loose cairns to show others where we've been, or stack them formally into walls to mark our boundaries. We build our homes from them. We encourage plants to spread across them. We entertain our friends and family on top of them. We sometimes sit quietly and simply listen to the sound of water cascading over them.

Our relationship with rocks is as old as life itself.

Perhaps it's because a single stone contains so much natural history. Or maybe we simply respect its heft and weight and want to glean some strength from its inherent solidity. A stone held in the hand feels like a piece of time made concrete.

Whatever the reason, humans—and other living creatures—have a natural affinity for stone. In this book, we celebrate the partnership of people and rocks by exploring some of the ways stone inspires men and women to use their imaginations—as well as their hands and backs—to create stunning exterior landscapes from a raw material nature has generously provided.

—*Laurel Saville*

PART ONE:
STONEWORK IDEAS AND INSPIRATION

A blond retaining wall curves into the distance, creating a functional lawn area and drawing the gaze out toward the distant landscape.

Chapter 1

STONE WALLS

THE NEW ENGLAND POET Robert Frost famously wrote, "Something there is that doesn't love a wall." Yet, stone walls *are* attractive to lichens, mosses, chipmunks, reptiles, and perhaps, most especially, homeowners. While Frost was referring to natural forces that cause stones to tumble from their placement, a well-built and gently maintained stone wall can sustain its rough beauty, timeless aesthetic, and rugged functionality for hundreds of years.

The earliest stone walls were often the result of farmers clearing land to be plowed. Today's walls are highly crafted landscape elements; they can be used to retain a slope and sculpt the land, making formerly unusable areas more functional and traversable. Stone walls can be used with other garden elements—for example, to support or surround a patio, create a planting area, or frame a deck. They also define borders, whether alongside a driveway or in a distant field. With their inherent contrast of soothingly colored natural material and weighted formality, stone walls add a feeling of permanence, solidity, and visual pause to the landscape of almost any home.

At the Chelsea Flower Show in England, a sand-colored stone wall makes an elegant backdrop for the mauve blooms and soft gray stems of lavender.

The Geological History of Stone Walls in New England

In his fascinating book *Stone by Stone*, Robert M. Thorson traces the provenance of the stone walls that lace the New England landscape back beyond the farmers who made them, all the way to the ice age of 15,000 to 30,000 years ago. As glaciers came down from the north and then receded, they scattered stones across the region. These were buried beneath centuries of decaying organic material that became soil. There, the stones waited for changes in human uses of the land to make themselves known. "Stone walls lie at the intersection of science and history, which became woven together during the transformation of wilderness into family farms," notes Thorson, a professor of geology and geophysics.

As pioneers began to clear the temperature-moderating forests, the exposed ground was subject to deeper freezing, which led to the upheaval of stones during thaw cycles, Thorson explains. The open areas were also more susceptible to erosion, which exposed yet more stones. Early stone walls were not built for ornamentation but rather were simply "magnets for the stone refuse that otherwise would have ended up in piles," he concludes.

The similarity of walls in England and New England is a result of these two parts of the world once being connected as a single continent, with similar cycles of weather and land development.

It wasn't until the early eighteenth century in the United States, according to Thorson, that "many primitive walls were rebuilt into more architecturally pleasing forms, especially on prosperous farms and estates.... With cash, labor, and a copious supply of stone already in place, hundreds of thousands of walls were built and rebuilt throughout the region."

So the next time you're wandering in the woods and come across the remnants of a stone wall coursing through the trees that have grown up around it, knocking bits of the rocks free with marauding roots and downed limbs, pause for a moment to consider the history, both geological and human, contained within the stones.

Stone by Stone: The Magnificent History of New England's Stone Walls, Robert M. Thorson (New York: Walker, 2002)

This wall was originally built in 1775 on what is now Winvian Farm in Litchfield, Connecticut. More than 200 years of wind, weather, and the beauty of gray-green lichen have softened its contours, but gravity and the skill of the original mason have allowed the wall to maintain a solid presence in the landscape.

There are two general categories of stone walls: dry laid and mortared. Dry-laid walls make use of gravity, the shapes of the stones, and the skill of the waller to form a stable wall; mortared walls use concrete to hold the stones in place. Dry-laid walls are usually stacked, with square stones laid in courses that support one another, although less formal effects can be achieved with piled walls, which make use of rounded boulders and stones. Mortared walls are a little more forgiving to create, as they are less reliant on the perfect placement of each stone. They are virtually indestructible, which makes them appropriate for high-use applications, such as steps. Mortared walls can also incorporate a wide variety of materials, such as pebbles, tiles, marbles, shells, and more, to create a mosaic effect, and with skill, they can be made to look remarkably like traditional dry-laid walls. But they take longer to build because you have to wait for the mortar to set up, and if you make a mistake placing a stone, well, it's cast in concrete. Many purists feel the only way to achieve the true, iconic stone wall aesthetic is to forego the cement.

▼ American's largest restored Shaker community, Pleasant Hill, has more than 25 miles (40.2 km) of stone fences such as this one, featuring striking vertical stone coping along the top.

▶ This section of wall from Pleasant Hill Shaker Village in Kentucky has been in place long enough that trees have rooted, grown up in its foundation, and now provide shelter and stability to the old stones.

TOOLS OF THE TRADE

ANDREA MORGANTE'S STONE WALL grew out of her civic efforts in her town, Hinesburg, Vermont. "I wrote a grant for the town to get a sidewalk installed that would extend from the main street to the post office," she explains. A professional landscaper, she realized the installation of a sidewalk would change the contours in front of her home. "When I moved here in 1978," she explains, "there was a steep slope down to the road, and I immediately planted a tall hedge, as this was an overgrown farmhouse with twenty junk cars that I was also turning into a landscaper's yard, with plant stock, trucks, and all the rest." She got the grant for the sidewalk and then set to work putting her own house in order.

"I cut down the hedge, and all of a sudden, people could see what a wreck my house was," she laughs. "The hedge had been there for almost twenty years." Morgante had a variety of stones left over from projects she'd done for clients around the state, including native field stone, Panton stone, and Wilmington stone. In anticipation of her project, she also collected stone from a neighbor's

field in exchange for helping with maple sugaring chores.

"I'd never do this for a client," Morgante says. "I'd only want to use stone indigenous to the site, not all these different stones with different geological formations. But I figured if it looked horrible, I'd just plant vines to cover it."

LOCAL COLOR

Morgante enlisted a local mason, David "Stoney" Mason. "He wanted to put a wheel in the stone wall," Morgante says. "I didn't have a wheel, but I did have a wheelbarrow.

I thought at first he was kidding, but he put it in, made it look like it was full of stone, and put a ledge over it so water doesn't get into the wheelbarrow and it doesn't rust. Then I dragged out a bunch of broken tools, and people started stopping by and dropping things off, so we decided to call it 'Tools of the Trade.' I even thought about putting a truck in the wall, but I decided that was getting a little carried away."

Landscape designer Andrea Morgante cobbled together stones left over from job sites, gathered from a neighbor's field, and scavenged from landscapers' yards—along with tools left behind in a shed—to create a wall that is a testament to her vocation.

Mason, she says, would just grab things out of her shed while she was away working on other job sites, so the completed wall ended up including shovels, rakes, a level, a pair of loppers, a chainsaw, a winch, old bricks, a teakettle, a watering can, and, eventually, even her son's toy cars. The wall managed to absorb all the stone in her yard—as well as some scavenged from other landscapers' yards—and Morgante had to buy only a few extra for the winding steps leading from the sidewalk.

Throughout the process, Morgante worked as the tender, helping select stones and ensuring visual continuity from one type of stone to another. "I like using a variety of sizes of stone," she notes. "Some people want walls that are consistent, with very tight joints, but I don't like that as much because it seems like you're not taking the natural stone and using it as you find it. You want to let each stone speak for itself." The result is a stunning pastiche, a stone-and-found-object patchwork that has become the talk of the town. "Some people think I'm nuts," Morgante says, "but most people seem to like it."

Andrea Morgante's Advice for Building a Stone Wall

"Building a wall is not the same as stacking stones. The art of a wall is understanding the relationships between the stones. What you're trying to get is something that reads in its entirety but is made up of many smaller pieces."

—A.M.

• The base is the most important thing; you have to have really good drainage. Is there groundwater? Will water build up behind the wall and push the stones outward? You might have to put in drainage pipes.

• Don't scrimp on the amount of stone you have. Get a big enough supply that you can pick and choose as you build, so you're not forced to use what's not quite right. What works in one place might not work someplace else.

• It's important to understand how the wall will fit in with the rest of the landscape and what the site calls for, depending on whether you have a modern house, a rambling farmhouse, or a typical suburban house.

• Don't build walls too tall; terrace them instead. Also, the relationship of the size of the stone to the size of the wall is important. You don't want big stones in small walls.

• Remember that walls take maintenance. Chipmunks, squirrels, and snakes make their homes in stone walls. Arrange your plantings around the idea that you're building condos for chipmunks.

• To be a good builder, you have to focus on what you're doing in the moment. You must visualize the space you have to fill together with the stone you have, and consider which face of the stone should be showing. It helps to have big hands and a strong back. And patience is really important. Be willing to try something and pull it out if it doesn't work.

At Holker Hall in Cumbria, United Kingdom, an annual exhibition and festival celebrates "Gardens, Countryside, and Food." This dry stone walling demonstration points out the importance of several of Morgante's wall-building tips, including having a good selection of stone to work with, as well as "big hands and a strong back."

A tall wall and wide walk keep the focus on the entry garden and front door instead of the nearby garage and parking area.

A MORE CONTEMPORARY
POINT OF VIEW

FOR THIS HILLSIDE PROJECT, Keith Wagner, a landscape architect in Burlington, Vermont, was hired to redo the gardens around a home in a contemporary style. The owner is an art collector, especially of outdoor sculpture, and he wanted to create a series of outdoor rooms as well as a terrace for large parties and entertaining.

The 10-acre (4 hectare) site in the midst of a 60-acre (24.2 hectare) property featured a large meadow, a mature woodlot, two ponds, a guest house, and beautiful views of majestic hillsides and Vermont's tallest peak, Mount Mansfield. Wagner describes the home itself as a "contemporary interpretation of a farmhouse," with some existing stone walls. However, a recent addition to the house rendered the walls "incoherent," so they were taken down and the stone stockpiled. While the "thin, slate-ish type of stone is not my favorite material," Wagner says, "he had a bunch of it, so we said, 'let's reuse it.'"

Wagner, an artist and fan of contemporary minimalism (one of his oversize metal ball sculptures graces the meadow near the larger of the two ponds), favors bold strokes and strong patterns that create rhythm and flow—essential to making a statement that can stand on its own in such a striking landscape.

A series of parallel walls bisected with a blond arcing wall makes a statement in an already dramatic landscape and draws the eye outward toward the mountains.

The buff-colored edging and walls accent the lighter tones in the more imposing gray walls, lending unity as well as visual relief to the massive areas of patio and paving.

"We tend to use hardscape as the skeleton for design," Wagner says. "A lot of the walls are about adding repetition to the landscape. Stone became the material that tied all of the elements together." Several walls define key functional areas; the most notable are parallel constructions jutting into the landscape, intersected and contrasted by a lower, buff-colored, arcing wall. "There's a big arc along one side of the house that looks out over the meadow toward the mountains," Wagner explains. "The arc contains all the usable terraced space. The repetition of the parallel walls creates a visual cadence that takes your eyes out to the meadow and beyond."

Other stone walls on the property control traffic, both human and vehicular. One wall runs parallel to the entry walkway so visitors focus on the garden rather than the nearby garage door. Slender walls are used "like parking strips to hint at where you're supposed to park," Wagner notes. "The walls become this repetitive theme, acting as guideposts for people."

Walkways function as another repeating theme. "They puncture through one space to another," Wagner says, "and are used like runners of a carpet that link the outdoor rooms." The theme continues farther from the house with a walkway that appears to jut directly into an existing pond. Another walkway takes people to an overlook at the edge of the meadow.

COLORFUL CONTINUITY

Meanwhile, more blond stone is used on the primarily bluestone terraces to create continuity. "If you look at the thin wall stone, it has hints of the yellow color in it," Wagner notes. "We were trying to tie the ground plain subtly to the walls. Some of that grounding, plain, dark gray stone also has a rust color in it, which ties the horizontal to the vertical surfaces." While the gray stone walls and bluestone patio are all dry laid, the buff-colored walls are concrete veneered. "They're retaining walls, so we needed the extra strength," says Wagner.

In addition to managing the grade changes and figuring out how "to make those spaces flow in an elegant way," Wagner also had to come up with a creative solution to a sudden about-face in one aspect of the plan. The owner had originally wanted a pool but changed his mind after the hole was dug and the concrete was poured. Instead of ripping out all this fresh work, Wagner suggested just filling it in, pointing out it would cost less and be simpler to go back to the original idea if the winds shifted again. He finished this trapezoidal intrusion into the landscape with grass and a lead-coated, copper-edged planting bed that contains a mass of blue fescue. "It's a kind of tongue-in-cheek nod to what was supposed to be blue pool water," Wagner chuckles.

A walkway crosses a patio and steps down to become a launching pad directly into the larger of two ponds that grace the property. At the same time, it directs the eye upward toward the hills.

WINDING **WALL**

Using computer graphics that appear to be watercolor, John Shaw-Rimmington illustrates his "Curvy Wall" before embarking on the actual building. "I like to visualize what the project is going to look like," he notes.

JOHN SHAW-RIMMINGTON, president of the Dry Stone Wall Association of Canada, is a fan of Andy Goldsworthy, the famed British artist who creates site-specific—and often impermanent—land art, sculptures, and installations using natural materials. While converting a couple of brick chimneys into stone for the owner of over 100 acres (40.5 hectares) near Lake Ontario, he left a copy of a Goldsworthy book with the client. In it were pictures of Goldsworthy's famous "Wall That Went on a Walk," installed at the Storm King Art Center in New York. "I knew I'd dangled a carrot in front of him," Shaw-Rimmington says. "And then there was that one fateful moment where he said, 'What's to stop me from having a curvy wall?'" Shaw-Rimmington realized that while Goldsworthy may have designed and created a stunning version of a winding stone wall, he didn't own the idea of it. "After all," Shaw-Rimmington notes, "any

wall, if it isn't straight, is curvy." So there was no reason he and his client couldn't make a site-specific curving stone wall of their own.

"We caught on to the idea that a wall need not be on a perimeter or a border that defines where your property turns into something else," says Shaw-Rimmington. "It's a feature, and so it can determine its own path." After walking the property and laying out garden hoses, they chose a placement that "maximizes what the wall can do for you visually and aesthetically. It was the first wall I've built where you can't stand back and see the whole thing because you lose it through the trees and then see it again. At first, this was frustrating, but then I realized the wall incorporated *time* as well as space. It told a story within the forest. The wall invites you to walk along it to discover more about it. It's an unraveling of sorts," Shaw-Rimmington explains.

From above, the wall creates a surprising yet natural symbiosis of stone, trees, and slope that invites exploration.

COPING WITH TRADITION

In addition to choosing local stone, they also decided to add upright coping, an element typical on English walls but not present on the Goldsworthy source of inspiration. "If you put up flat stones across the top, you have pieces that are easy to push off," Shaw-Rimmington points out. "But if you take those same flat pieces and turn them sideways, you have them leaning against their neighbors and they tighten up because there is greater downward

To create a proper base that ensures drainage and a good footing, Shaw-Rimmington and fellow waller Dean McLellan excavate to a depth of 6 inches (15.2 cm) and then fill the shallow trench with ³/₄-inch (1.9 cm) clear crushed gravel before beginning to build. This process also allows them to see the exact footprint of the wall.

The wall in progress shows John Shaw-Rimmington selecting stones, as well as a break opening to a footpath that flows down the hillside. Note the vertical coping in the process of being set on the completed section of the wall.

pressure per volume. No stone can be pulled out without dislodging the one next to it. It looks precarious, but it's not, and it discourages kids and animals from running across the top."

This gravitational pull is part of what makes dry walling so endlessly appealing to Shaw-Rimmington. "As soon as you add cement to a wall, the whole thing is dead and locked in," he says. "But when you can see that all these stones were placed individually and are held here by their own weight and friction, the wall has a very human element. And a stone wall looks great at every stage of its life. Even an unfinished wall looks like it has been there a long time. Each phase of a wall's life displays something attractive and timeless. Even a simple pile of stone is asking you to get involved."

The curving wall certainly begs for involvement. It's visible from the driveway as you approach the house, then goes over a hill and is intermittently obscured by trees. "You can catch a glimpse of it, but then you have to go and explore," Shaw-Rimmington suggests. The best view? "Well, it's one you'll never get," he says. "I once went up on the roof of the house to take a picture of the whole thing. And that was pretty spectacular."

A closeup of one of the wall's many sinewy bends demonstrates how the stones must be placed level to ensure stability, even though the ground underneath slopes in a different direction.

Shaw-Rimmington also made an arched gateway as an entrance to a nature trail on the same property as the curving wall. Employing an old barn foundation, local fieldstones, and glacial granite, he used a form of sand piled on top of a table and a plywood semicircle to support the arch while he built it. "I love the look of round and square working together. It makes you look outside the pattern," he says. "A wall with only square stones does not look anywhere near as interesting as one that combines shapes." The natural shrubbery cascades over the gateway in the summertime, creating an inviting entrance where "you can't even tell where the wall stops."

ROCKSWIRL

KEN MILLS HAS BEEN a custom furniture builder, restaurant owner, biochemist, marketing consultant, multimedia arts presenter, and, more recently, landscape designer. "It seems like a leap," he says, "but they all have to do with design and presentation, especially spatial presentation, and I look at landscaping as choreography, performance, a dance, really. This is how I approach everything. It's design and presentation trying to influence an emotional reaction."

For the backyard of this compact home in an old neighborhood just outside of Burlington, Vermont, Mills faced a problem not frequently encountered on stage but nevertheless solved by means of the tried-and-true artistic approach of trial, error, and improvisation. "The backyard was wet, with heavy clay soils, and it sloped toward the house," Mills recalls. "It was always mushy off the back

steps." The homeowners wanted a place where they could entertain and enjoy the backyard, but they didn't want a deck. The patio, Mills says, was obvious. The wall came from long conversations and the process of trying to solve a serious problem suddenly made manifest.

A huge rainstorm was the catalyzing event. "I thought the water would be no problem after we had sloped the grade appropriately away from the house, but then, lo and behold, this entire huge hole where the patio was going to be was filled with water not going anywhere. It was a lake." This is where the improvisation came in. "You think it's an insurmountable problem, so much worse than we imagined," Mills laughs, "but then you come up with a solution, and it becomes very exciting. It was one of those situations where a problem becomes an opportunity."

A bowling ball was repurposed as a decorative item as well as a convenient means to hold down the dry well cover. The homeowners thus retain access to the sump pump for regular maintenance.

What began as an effort to make a muddy backyard more usable turned into a project that required everything from civil engineering and inventive drainage techniques to a creative use of stone and a recreational item.

The first step was to see what was underneath the clay. "We dug down a few feet, hoping to hit sand," but without luck, Mills recalls. "The whole area is flat; there's no obvious place to drain anything, but we had to get rid of the water." At first he tried a dry well, but that proved insufficient. The next step was a sump pump in the dry well that runs year round and puts the water directly into the home's front yard—which, strangely enough, is consistently too dry. "So then we had this area where the dry well was. We needed access to maintain the sump pump and kept asking how could we disguise it so it would look like it's there for a reason."

BRING ON THE BRAINSTORM

"We thought, let's build a wall around it. And that's when we came up with the idea of a continuous, circling wall." Then Mills and the owners thought it would be great to add a firepit. And then also a garden space outside the patio—which led to the idea of a wall that "rises up out of the patio and then falls back again," Mills says. "I like the idea of curvature that moves in multiple directions, rising and falling as well as curving horizontally, and also playing with the perception of walls that pass through instead of running into one another to create an infinity symbol. Then you get into fire and water, with life in the center, and you can extend the metaphor as far as you want."

The concept was put down on paper as an architectural drawing ahead of time. "There are always things that change on site and an evolution of how the details fit together. There's always a bit of letting go," Mills adds. And, often, happy surprises. The diamond-shaped seat was the result of simply seeing "a big flat boulder I thought would be great to use somehow. I like the idea of something irregular intruding on something perfectly constructed. It is a huge piece of natural stone surrounded by the perfect rectangles and squares of the patio."

The circular object set in the middle of a swirl of stone wall looks like a bowling ball because it *is* a bowling ball; it holds down the hatch to the dry well. Its shape is echoed in a sister swirl with the small circle of a firepit.

The patio is made of bluestone and the wall is predominantly Corinthian granite, chosen for its comple-

The circular shape of the dry well is duplicated at the other end of the swirl with a round firepit, giving the whole area multiseason, multipurpose usability.

The landscape designer made the most of the challenging circumstances to create a wall whose fluidity belies its difficult beginnings as well as the heft and geometry of its stones.

This patio and wall bring together the elements of fire, water, rock, and plants in a unified composition wherein each feature flows through the stone to every other.

mentary colors. "It has a purplish sheen to it, and some rust," Mills notes. "We didn't want all the stone to be the same. We went and looked at about twenty kinds of stone, and this is the one that stood out."

While the design process may sound a bit New Age in approach, the installation faced serious, down-to-earth challenges. In addition to the water problem, there was an access problem: only one narrow way to get into the backyard, which severely restricted movement of workers,

machinery, and materials. "It was difficult to turn around, and you had to make sure you didn't paint yourself into a corner," Mills recalls. "During the building, I was wondering how it would turn out, but on nearly every project, there's this moment during the last few days where all of a sudden, it's like, 'Wow!'"

Chapter 2

STONE PATIOS AND ENTERTAINING AREAS

IT'S DURABLE, ATTRACTIVE, easy to clean, and shrugs off the weather. Natural stone is an ideal material for creating outdoor entertaining areas that are functional and attractive and that become the groundwork for other exterior elements, from planters bursting with exuberant blooms to perennial borders, from clipped lawns to natural, wildflower-strewn meadows. Not to mention spas, pools, fireplaces, grills, and outdoor kitchens.

Outdoor entertaining areas usually are organized around some kind of stone "carpeting" that serves to define the space. Paving stones are available in many colors and a variety of precut sizes and shapes—and as natural, unfinished pieces as well, of course. The right angles and precise sizing of precut pavers make them easier to install, in either formal and random patterns. Joints can be made tight to reduce the incidence of weeds and to ease maintenance. Natural stones create a more informal look, as if the stones were perhaps simply uncovered in place. Less organized placement

A boulder-strewn hillside provides a rugged backdrop for an outdoor kitchen complete with a gas range and a pizza oven built to appear as if they were carved from the stone itself.

and larger gaps provide opportunities to use creeping plants, herbs, and ground covers to soften the rock edges, scent the air as you walk, or even improve the flavor of food on the grill. Gravel, which comes in many shades, sizes, and shapes, can also be used underfoot; install weed barrier fabric before bringing in the gravel to keep plants from cropping up where they're not wanted.

Especially in areas where winter ensures a freeze-and-thaw cycle, most patios are built on a base of compacted gravel and a layer of sand or rock dust that allows the stones to shift and move along with the seasons. Regular maintenance may include lifting and resetting a stone that has heaved a bit too high or sunk a bit too low.

Building a patio with concrete may be sturdier in the short run, but cracking, splitting, and starting over are likely if you live in a cold climate.

While stone has always been the material of choice for patios and walkways, valued for its durability and good looks, new materials, better products, and simplified installation means stone can also be used in more and more interesting ways in the exterior landscape. In seats, facings, copings, firepits, countertops, and tables, stone provides strength and elegance. The hidden surprises described in the following projects now make stone more comfortable in all seasons as well.

A series of open, slatted gates creates a feeling of privacy in this patio while keeping the views open for guests dining al fresco. A gravel edge enhances the shape of the space and keeps occasional raindrops from splashing.

A quiet dining area invites visitation with sandy, seaside colors in stonework. Lilac-colored wildflowers and ornamental grasses wave in the ocean breezes.

RE-CREATING NATURE

THE FIRST TIME George Workman toured the land on which he had been hired to create a family compound, he felt like he was walking in a swamp. "The groundwater dynamics were challenging because there were a few surface streams, but most of the water was groundwater traveling through a thin layer of very fine, sandy soil over clay," explains Workman, landscape architect and owner of Landworks Design in Newcastle, Maine, "On the western side of the property are the granite formations of the Camden Hills, and all the runoff comes down these hills into the ocean. The highly volatile outwash soils are continuous from Belfast to Rockland. Recently, a 5-acre (2 hectare) property in nearby Rockland collapsed into the ocean."

From these 10 damp acres (4 hectares), Workman was to create a dazzling and complex landscape and playground. The architects had sited the house high on the hill to maximize views, but a side effect was that the house was "basically damming the groundwater coming down off the mountains," Workman said. "Drainage engineering became the biggest issue. I wanted to make everything seem as natural as possible, so we had to reform what would have happened naturally, dry everything out, and still get all the runoff to drain into the sea. The owner's request was that she be able to walk to shore barefoot and not get her feet wet."

These quite literally underlying issues became the impetus for the design. "The house was conceived as an English manor house, and I wanted to complement the stonework and the layout of the house with a design of

▶ A huge range of stonework in patios, walls, walks, steps, and pattern creates a variety of living, relaxing, dining, and swimming spaces, all reflective of, and inspired by, the rocky Maine coast.

The scale of the site, along with the desire to have the pool and walls seem to emerge from natural ledge, made using extremely large stones a requirement.

equal scale," Workman says. The first step was to create level areas in the sloping hillside where patios, lawns, and a pool could be sited. "To accomplish this, I came up with the idea of bringing in faux ledge as a way to augment nature," Workman explains. "We took ledge from another site and brought it to this one to make it look like the house was built on natural ledge." The next step was to build walls on top of the ledge with stone similar to the type used in the home's chimneys. "By building the stone walls over the faux ledge, we created the impression that the ledge had always been there," he says.

FRACTAL GEOMETRY

With the basic structural elements in place, Workman combined his own theories of design with a handful of the owner's childhood experiences to create a unique layout for the patio and pool, full of surprises waiting to be discovered. The apparently random pattern of the patio pavers is anything but. "I base my design approach on the theory of fractals," Workman says, "which suggests that any part of any natural system is a replication of its own form. It's a scientific term that says anything you see in nature looks like an outgrowth of its tiniest part. When I design with stone to create a naturalistic ledge, I study the geological formation of the extended region, and then I find a place of similar geologic consistency from which to borrow the stone for the faux ledge. From that, I reconfigure the stone into the same geologic disposition and geometry it has in nature."

Workman began by placing the ledge formations in a north-south trend, so they appear as an outcropping of the regional geologic foundation. His next move was just a bit more complicated. "The design of the patios represents an abstraction of a microscopic look at a piece of granite. It's as if you cut through a piece of granite and looked at the crystalline structure," Workman says.

He had masons code, template, and cut stone to his exact design, so when they arrived on site they could be fit together like a jigsaw puzzle. "When I designed the patio," Workman says, "I named every piece of stone." He also paid special attention to the patio's orientation; it had to fit with the geometry of the house. "I didn't want to put

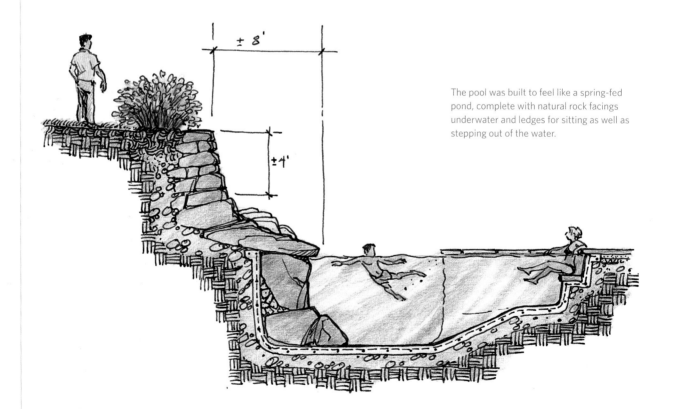

The pool was built to feel like a spring-fed pond, complete with natural rock facings underwater and ledges for sitting as well as stepping out of the water.

a railing around the patio, so in order to meet code requirements, I had to add a lower shelf below the patio wall. That way, the danger of inadvertently stepping off the patio in the wrong place was caught by a lower perimeter planter. And all of this was done so I could create the sensation of standing on the bow of a ship, looking out to sea; I wanted to create an exhilarating experience from the apex of the patio as everything falls away around you."

CHILDHOOD REVISITED

The pool below the ship's prow is designed to be reminiscent of the adventure, playfulness, and discovery of childhood. "Every move I made was with the thought in mind that this is a family compound, and they have a long-term Maine connection, so the pool had to relate to the places the owner remembered as a child, like her favorite swimming hole," Workman recalls. "I went there and looked around so I could re-create the parts that were special, including that sense of discovery in naturally occurring pools and streams." He made sure to embed some surprises as well. There's an outdoor shower hidden in the rocks and a place for jumping off the rock into

the pool, just as one might find in a pool deep in the woods at a secret location. There's even a cave below the ledge of the pool that hides not only the pool mechanicals but also the unexpected treasure of a painting. Even the plantings were designed to appear as if they occurred naturally. "I take my cues from what's already there," Workman says. "The farther you are from the house, the more native the plantings are."

This is a landscape expertly crafted to appear as if it had grown organically. "It's about the Maine cottage experience," Workman says. "It was about paying careful attention to the clients' sensibility, needs, and affections, and being thoughtful about what they love about Maine, how they're going to use the space, and blending art with function."

The massive amount of stonework used around this home is softened and relieved by the selection of different shapes and sizes of rocks, a variety of terraces, and the addition of creeping plants that drift over and around the hard edges of a stairway.

The stonework includes many surprises to be discovered, including a jumping-off point, an outdoor shower, and a grotto that hides pool mechanicals and provides a place to play hide and seek.

STONES ALONG THE WATER

"THERE'S A LOVE-HATE RELATIONSHIP with lakefront property in Chicago," notes Douglas Hoerr of Douglas Hoerr Landscape Architecture in Chicago. "You love being perched there, but on those days when it's stormy and gray, it can be gloomy and threatening." For this property overlooking the Wilmette Harbor on Lake Michigan, Hoerr's job was to turn what had been a fair amount of apprehension into unobstructed love. An existing ranch house on a ½-acre (0.2 hectare) lot had been expanded and modified to resemble the shingled cottages the owner remembered from her childhood back east. However, with only 15 feet (4.6 m) between the back of the house and a steep slope to a concrete wall that functioned as a shoreline, winter storms sent freezing spray up onto the house and turned the backyard into a skating rink that led right onto the lake. "Something had to be done to dampen the wave impact and give the house

What was once a daunting and sometimes forbidding shoreline was made hospitable with stonework that breaks up the waves, provides a secure backdrop, and carves out a sheltered sitting area.

A comforting, curving stairway made of New York State fieldstone set in grout and surrounded by sturdy walls leads from the house and gardens to the lake.

a psychological sense of security," Hoerr says, "and there's nothing like stone walls to make you feel more secure."

In this case, it was actually a series of stone walls. Working with the Army Corps of Engineers, the U.S. Environmental Protection Agency, and specialized contractors, Hoerr's design called for destroying the existing concrete wall, raising the seawall by about 4 feet (1.2 m), installing 300 tons (272 metric tons) of boulders to dampen the wave impact, and then creating a concrete catwalk and sitting area surrounded by a soothing wall of New York State fieldstone artistically set in mortar. Meandering stone steps, a firepit, and a maritime-inspired open railing that does not obstruct the views completed the property-to-lake interface. Now the grandchildren are free to swim, water ski, and enjoy the sight of boats on the water while roasting marshmallows.

STONE JOINERY

However, this extensive shoreline engineering project was just the beginning of a complete site overhaul. Hoerr notes that in any landscape design, there are really three clients to consider: the homeowner, the house, and the site itself. In this case, all three had specific requirements. The homeowner wanted to extend the west-to-east transformation she'd done on her house to the entire property. "She said, 'I want a vegetable garden, and a spot for my

Almost all the stone used on the property is some form of granite or decomposed granite, such as this pea stone courtyard and garden, a choice that unites the many diverse functional areas and reflects a New England aesthetic.

grandkids, and a spot for my dog, and a cutting garden, and roses, and…'—so there was this overlay of desire on the project," Hoerr recalls. Meanwhile, the expansive house was very powerful, and the lot quite compact. Hoerr addressed these concerns by creating a series of discrete spaces and using stone to marry them. "Everything is granite or some form of decomposed granite," he says. "The stone was the first thing chosen to complement the East Coast architecture of the home. All the other materials were chosen in sympathy with that. Even the plants were chosen to have some sort of honest relationship back to that shingle-style home."

A sense of approach was developed with a curving cobblestone driveway made of hand-selected reclaimed granite street pavers from Chicago. This leads to an auto court of compacted gravel topped with pea stone, which is echoed in another gravel terrace out back. Bluestone distressed with sandblasting to remove its patina was used in the entry, a large porch, and patio. Walls of New York State fieldstone define and protect functional areas such

as the lawn and the vegetable garden. Large boulders from central Wisconsin are set among the plantings to give the entire area a naturalized authenticity that hearkens to its New England inspiration. "Typically, vernacular styles don't travel well," Hoerr says, "But in this case, it worked."

Part of what makes such a complex plan work on a small lot with a big house set on a dramatic lake is the confident use of equally strong elements: grand entry gates, stone walls, columns surrounding the porch, and strategically placed large trees. "You have to use garden architecture to make the house feel like it unfolds onto the lot," Hoerr says. "And you have to create foreground so you're not just looking out at a big, gray wall of the lake." It is through this "patterning and formation" of space that Hoerr was able to create a cohesive landscape that met so many practical, functional, aesthetic, and nostalgic demands. "You have to make sure all your decisions go back to the original concept," Hoerr says, "so it feels authentic and not gimmicky or cute."

An authentic and natural feeling is created with large stones, rugged plantings, and strong architectural elements.

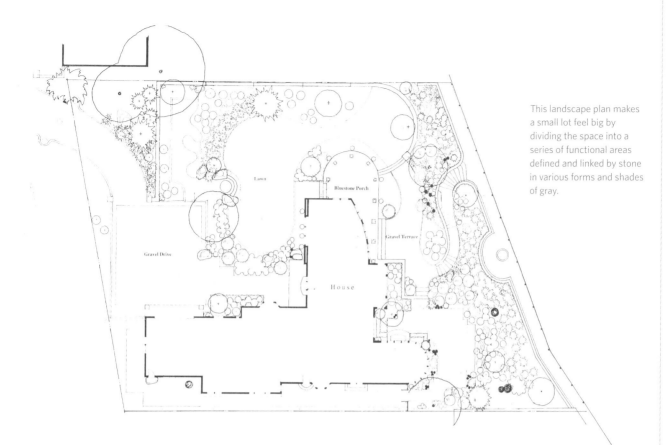

This landscape plan makes a small lot feel big by dividing the space into a series of functional areas defined and linked by stone in various forms and shades of gray.

The cobblestone driveway is made from granite pavers reclaimed from the Chicago streets and handpicked for consistency of color.

ITALIAN INSPIRATION

WHEN LANDSCAPE ARCHITECT Bob Hursthouse first met with these Chicago-area clients, they wanted to build a small patio space and to maximize the lawn outside their home as a play area for their children. He pointed out that the 1,200-square-foot (112 sq m) yard was too shady and small for a lawn. Then the homeowners went to Italy and came back with a different and more challenging request: to create an Italian piazza in their backyard.

"It's a rambling Arts and Crafts–style house," Hursthouse notes. "Not Italian at all. But I thought it was a

great inspiration and suggested we sit down and figure out the elements that make a piazza special and see which we could incorporate into a suburban backyard." The list included a large paved area, a dining area, a sense of enclosure, trickling water for a soothing auditory experience, and space that's equally comfortable for a small family group gathered for dinner at the end of a long day, or a party of twenty celebrating a holiday.

The once-wished-for lawn was quickly eliminated. As Hursthouse notes, "After the age of five, the days of

The pond feature is a compact surprise, tucked into a corner and surrounded by a sitting wall, with two brass founts that bring the soothing sound of trickling water to the landscape.

At 6 feet (1.8 m), this wall is too tall to be dry laid, but mortar is raked deep into the joints so it is invisible. Large rocks are set on edge to give visual relief and variety to the expanse of stone.

playing wiffle ball in the backyard are gone, and kids are off to organized sports." Instead, he suggested a bluestone patio, designed not only to be easily accessible from any of the six doors lining the back of the house but also to unify the disparate elements of home, yard, gardens, and accent features.

HEAT TO SMOOTH

The field of the patio is broken by three major elements: a dining table, a firepit, and a small pond. The dining area is defined by a large table of fabricated bluestone set on cast limestone plinths that anchor it and give it a sense of permanence. The bluestone for the top was quarried, cut, and given a thermal finish that "blows heat onto the surface of the stone to blister off irregularities so it's smooth but not polished," Hursthouse explains. "This keeps it from being slippery and evens out the irregularities that would cause a plate or glass to wobble." The columns—as well as all

the planters around the property—are made with a finely ground limestone gravel mixed with dry Portland cement and hand-packed into forms that then set up using nothing more than moisture in the surrounding air.

The firepit is given contrast and emphasis with a ring of porphyry, a reddish, igneous rock from the granite family that hearkens to the cobblestones of Italy. Its warm color complements the expanse of bluestone by heightening the subtle undertones in the paving. The ample diameter of the firepit, more than 6 feet (1.8 m), makes it a comforting destination for roasting hot dogs or marshmallows on cool evenings. For real outdoor cooking, the family uses a range set up around the corner, closer to the kitchen.

The water feature tucked into the corner was perhaps the most challenging aspect of the composition. "We went around and around on the design," says Hursthouse, "from a three-tier, 8-foot-tall (2.4 m) formal fountain to a raised

A large firepit reportedly gets even more use than the living room fireplace, no matter the season or weather. An outdoor range for real cooking is set up around the corner, near the inside kitchen.

hot tub, and then scaled it down to a recessed water garden with a sitting wall that offers a bit of a surprise." Only 4 feet (2 m) square, the small pond features two brass founts that provide a "real clean, simple way to handle the movement of the water," he concludes. As a bonus, "the wall behind extends to the floor of the pond, so as you look down and in, you see stonework in the water among the aquatic plants and fish."

The most dramatic part of the landscape is the walls that enclose this suburban piazza. At 6 feet (1.8 m) high, they are too tall to be built using dry-laid techniques. But Hursthouse achieved the traditional effect by raking the mortar deep among the Pennsylvania fieldstones so it is invisible to passers-by. To alleviate the extreme expanse of the wall, Hursthouse used the variety inherent in the stones themselves. "The seam face is exposed as it would be in nature," he explains, "and in some places we've turned and exposed the bed face of a rock so it looks like a boulder. This breaks up the mass of the wall and adds detail and texture."

PATH TO NOWHERE

Intrigue is achieved with an opening that intentionally leads nowhere. "The problem with enclosing a garden is that there's no way out," says Hursthouse. "But this opening provides a vista, a peek-through." On the other side of the wall, green space between the homes and a large planter creates a visual stopping point in the midst of the vista. To increase the sense of enclosure even more—and add height where code restrictions limit the wall to 6 feet (1.8 m)—Hursthouse added a trellis on top. "It creates an overhead canopy, a third dimension."

As he considers this home now, Hursthouse finds the most satisfying aspect of the installation is that it actually is used. "We took the time to distill the Italian piazza, and instead of creating an Italian garden, we figured out the feelings that were most important to them. Now, as I walk the space, there's always somewhere else for me to go, a different vantage point, a different feeling. The family uses the space a lot. And that's really satisfying. Too many things are built that are never used."

The patio and other elements in this landscape were inspired by the piazzas discovered by the homeowners on a trip to Italy. To make the concept work in a suburban setting, the architect distilled and replicated a piazza's key components and the benefits they confer.

A STUDY IN **SIMPLICITY**

THIS PROPERTY IN LAKE FOREST, Illinois, is an amalgam of styles, gardens, and buildings, the result of joining two adjacent properties. In addition to the traditionally-styled main residence, the grounds include a great lawn, a series of gardens and paths, a pool, two English Tudor changing rooms, and a Japanese tea room. When the owners called landscape architects Rocco Fiore & Sons and asked them to plan an Asian garden in the midst of all these other elements, the critical challenge was to create something that united the various vernaculars. As landscape architect Drew Johnson notes, "There was already a conflict of architecture, and we didn't want to design a garden that created more conflict."

The well-traveled homeowners were passionate about Asian themes, art, and design. They also wanted to "celebrate traditional elements of fire, water, wind, light, color, texture, and a sense of openness," according to Rocco Fiore's website. "Harmonizing these elements would come only from simplification...restraint, dignity, and composure." The design evolved through close consultation with the homeowners, who shared books and photographs illustrating their favored elements.

While the installation is called an Asian discovery garden, it includes very few plants. It is a rock and stone garden in the most literal sense. Beds are filled with Arkansas washed gravel that is more angular than

A pair of gates, open in design and function, invites a visitor to enter into an Asian-inspired garden that offers minimalist serenity and creature comfort. The garden also works as a quiet refuge and unifying element to what is otherwise a large and complex landscape of buildings and gardens in differing styles.

The patio—which includes heated benches, a firepit, and a spa for multiseason usability—connects the disparate architecture of a teahouse, pool house, and veranda.

rounded and can be raked into elegant patterns, as is common in traditional Asian gardens. The borders are made of lannonstone from Wisconsin that has been cut and tumbled to soften the edges. Between the pale lannonstones is a contrasting ribbon of black river rock. The bluestone paving "has a relationship to the pool area," notes Johnson. "Then we carried the same angles and lines of bluestone and brick through the garden and the rest of the property, picking it up again on the other side of the pool pavilion."

ESSENTIAL GROUNDWORK

Most of these foundational elements, other than the edging, are set on 8 inches (20.3 cm) of gravel topped with 2 inches (5 cm) of sand. Johnson points out, "We do everything dry laid to accommodate freeze-and-thaw cycles. It's

a lot easier to go back in and re-level a section of a patio from time to time than to deal with cracks and tuckpointing. Concrete is always going to crack, which, long term, means you end up with more repair costs. With dry-laid work, you may have a little bit of repair every year, but in concrete you have to go back after five years or so and possibly repair larger problems."

Vertical interest is created with a series of sculptural, gunmetal granite rocks set in the gravel. "We just brought out ten or so stones and began playing with them," Johnson explains. "We'd bring each one into the space to see if we liked it. Then we kept refining and reducing the number of stones in a process of simplification."

While this garden does have an element of soothing austerity, "the purpose of any space is to be used," Johnson

From the firepit, you can look past the patio to the calm field of raked gravel, artfully placed stones, and low shrubs that are key features of the garden and reflect the owners' love of Asian art and style.

points out. The design incorporates practical, functional elements that ensure human comfort during a variety of activities. The spa and firepit give homage, as the owners wanted, to the elements of water and fire, but they also encourage people to enjoy the area in any season. Benches are made of concrete honed to give it a smooth surface. The footings are stainless steel, a material also found in the teahouse. The firepit is hollow, with a self-contained bowl that holds a grouping of terra-cotta balls that provide visual interest even when the fire is not burning and that continue the rock and stone theme. Johnson especially appreciates the contrast of the ruddy stones and the dark soot that has given them an interesting patina and texture.

FOUR-SEASON COMFORT

The entire area underfoot and under the seating is heated—a feature most important to four-season usability and maintenance in northern climes. Johnson explains the mechanics: "There is a boiler system in back of the pavilion, and a system of coils about 9 inches (23 cm) apart runs through the whole site. This ¾-inch (2 cm) piping is set in a 2-inch (5 cm) sand bed and looped up into the benches. Hot water and antifreeze run through the coils, just like an old radiator system. Sensors in the stone detect the temperature so the system doesn't run constantly. It's just enough heat to keep the area warm, open, and dry so they can set their towels down."

There was a lot of experimentation and on-site design. "We marked things on the ground and walked the site to see how circulation would flow. We made cardboard cutouts of the benches and let them sit there for a few days, tweaking their position so we could be sure they worked." Much of this manipulation of materials resulted in a process of reduction and simplification that is at the heart of what makes this garden so successful on its own and as part of the larger property. "You don't have to do a lot or make things complicated," Johnson says. "It looks like a lot of things are happening, but only a few things are going on."

The overall plan shows how the bluestone paths, cross-hatched with brick, connect and unify the many preexisting elements in the landscape and help guide visitors from one garden area to another.

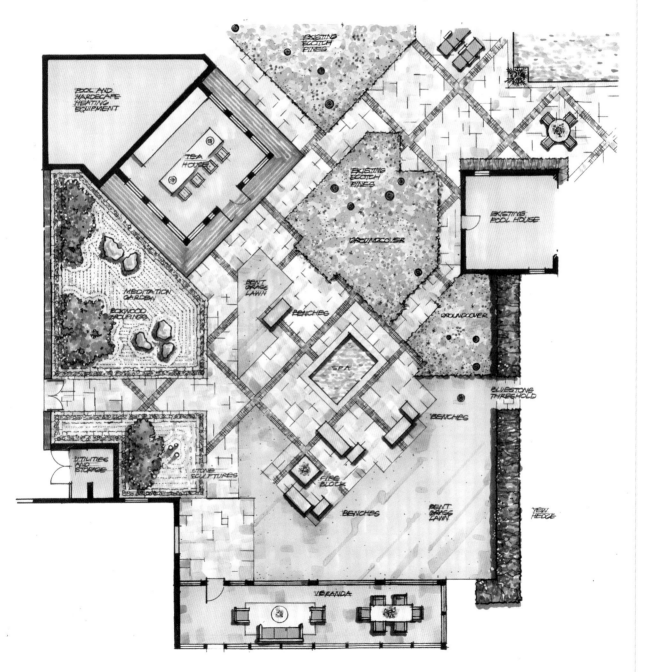

STONE AS FOUNDATION, STONE AS FAÇADE

MICHAEL GLASSMAN KNEW he had plenty of work to do to make this site in South Sacramento, California, a more usable space in the outdoor environment. "The site was just a tired and nonfunctional backyard with a little patch of lawn, ugly aggregate around the pool and patio, broken concrete, a dolphin fountain, and four half-dead trees," recalls Glassman, of Glassman & Associates.

The first decision was what *not* to do. "We knew we didn't want to use concrete," Glassman notes. "We wanted to use a more natural material." He chose Rox Panels from Rox® Pro for their natural and functional attributes. "It's real rock, but instead of having to do every piece one by one," Glassman explains, "it comes in prefab sheets that you adhere to concrete block. Because we did so much stonework, if you had to do it individually, it would have taken forever and been astronomically expensive. By building everything out of concrete block and rebar, you have structural integrity, but the Rox Panels give you this

A planter made from easily installed stone façade connects the kitchen to the pool and makes the entire space lush and inviting. Fencing is painted a gray similar to the patio for a neutral backdrop, while bursts of red flowers add a pop of color against the silvery fronds of ornamental grass.

wonderful, natural façade." And, he hastens to point out, you don't need to be a professional mason to use Rox Panels.

In the end, Glassman covered almost everything in the backyard with this natural façade. "We decided on that stone, and it started the theme," he notes. "I don't like composite or imitation stones because they fade over time. This won't fade, and I knew it came in ledge stone as well, so it worked everywhere." Plus, Glassman prefers continuity in his designs. "I like a flow. I don't like introducing ten materials," he says. "I wanted to unify materials and a color scheme, and bring it all through, with the hardscape becoming a backdrop for the accessories of the fountain, furniture, pool, and so on."

Because the Rox Panels product are not pavers, Glassman found random slate in similar color tones to use for the patio, coping, and planter capstones. The existing pool was updated with new tile and a pebbled finish to give it a more natural look. Instead of working around the older, not-very-attractive trees, Glassman added a raised planter with a waterfall to give the area visual and aural interest.

All the paving and stone surfaces succeeded in maximizing the most useful space for entertainment, which now includes an outdoor kitchen complete with an expansive grill and counters with seating. The countertops are finished in granite that not only matches the colors of the rest of the stone, but is used in the interior kitchen as well. "I'm a big one for inside-outside," Glassman notes. Umbrellas complete the inviting picture and give the area important multiweather functionality—which, in this warm, northern California location, means they provide shade more than protection from rain.

A soft color palette of buffs and grays creates continuity between the hardscape and the furniture. There is a variety of places to gather and socialize within the backyard.

TOO MUCH STONE?

Glassman confesses to a moment or two of concern over the sheer ubiquity of the stone. "There were a few times I worried whether we overdid the stone," he says. "But then we put in the plants, the furniture, and the fountains, and at that point it all came together." The plants are particularly important to the overall design and usability of the space. Not only does the planting material provide a counterpoint to the stone, but by using lots of planters and beds up around the house, the floor plan is kept open for people to gather and circulate. Plus, the plantings can be freshened throughout the season. "We used a lot of

interesting plant materials," Glassman points out, "with grasses and a lot of red and other rich, bright colors and textures to soften the stone."

The unity of the overall space was enhanced by artful decisions about pedestrian but necessary elements. Glassman ticks off several changes that were made on the fly: "There was an ugly garage door that we changed to a carriage door. Heat pumps and air conditioners were going to be moved, but we decided to screen them instead. There was a gray wood fence; it was new, so we stained it the color of the house for continuity." Glassman sees these additions and alterations as part of the creative process. "Even though we did plans and working drawings," he says, "as the project progressed, we made changes as

needed. You have to understand that with any landscape project, there are going to be changes, and it helps to be receptive to changes as the project goes on. If you get pigeonholed, your job will suffer."

Real stone in prefabricated panels makes it easy to create the look of hand-built, dry-laid stonework at a fraction of the cost and time.

Flowers and upright trees add color, vertical features, and textural softness to the large expanses of stone.

Michael Glassman's Advice for Outdoor Entertaining Areas

"For an outdoor kitchen, think in terms of how you'd plan for indoors. Make sure you have enough space to work, consider the layout of the amenities, decide what's important to include."

—M.G.

• Do you want a warming drawer, a barbecue, an oven? A refrigerator is one of the nicest things, to keep drinks on hand. If you can locate the sewer line, you can have running water and even an outdoor dishwasher.

• Have an area where people can sit and talk to you while you cook. Design the space so you face your company so people can hang out, talk, and get their dish.

• Try to use some of the same materials in your outdoor kitchen as you do inside to create continuity.

• Provide shade.

• Bigger is better. No one has ever complained about having too much space. Divide the space into rooms and create spaces for what you like to do.

• Don't bring lots of concrete and paving right up to the home, but soften it with planting. Use pots for accents. Include drainage under pots so dirty water doesn't get onto the patio. Run a drip tube into the pots so you don't have to be a slave to watering.

• Don't plant anything too tall near the barbecue. This is, however, a good place for herbs or citrus to use for cooking and garnishing.

• Try to use stone indigenous to the area. You don't want anything too slippery or that absorbs so much heat you could burn your feet. I like real rather than synthetic stone; synthetic stone has a tendency to lose its color, but natural stone lasts forever. Whenever you use natural materials, you'll get a nicer look.

This outdoor entertaining area provides places for a full range of activities, from dining to sunbathing, swimming to sitting by the firepit. Stone is used in a variety of elevations to draw the eye out as well as up.

Chapter 3

STONE AND WATER

ASIAN GARDENERS HAVE KNOWN for centuries that no landscape is complete with plants alone. It's essential to represent all the natural elements, including stone and water.

Adding a water element to your stonescape can be as simple as buying a sculptural element with a recirculating pump, easy to find at any home store. Garden centers often sell kits that range from a fountain that gently drips water over a decorative lip to a preformed pond complete with aquatic plants. If you want to create something much more elaborate, lots of information and guidance is available from companies that specialize in building ponds or helping homeowners figure out how to do it on their own. If you do decide to bring water into the garden, try to find a way to make it move. While looking at the smooth surface of water in a pond is quite tranquil, hearing it cascade over rocks or spout from a fountain gives pleasure of water an entirely new dimension.

Another consideration is how much water to use. Many people report, after adding a water feature, that they wish the pond were just a bit bigger, or the waterfall had one more level, or the foun-

In this Australian garden, fire, water, stone, and plants all work together in a compact space; here, a rivulet runs between a split slab of granite bisected by other pieces that mimic the shape of mountains.

tain had more of a presence among the perennials. While the fountain or pond sitting on the floor at the home center seems quite large, be sure to take measurements, lay out a hose in the yard, perhaps mock up something similar out of cardboard, and place it in the intended setting. This is the only way you can get a true sense of scale and how the garden components will work together.

Once you have a water feature, consider which plants and animals are appropriate to include. A large pond can be a wonderful home for koi, fish known to be smart and engaging enough to become pets. Many beautiful plants prefer damp conditions and can bring color, texture, and structure to the water feature.

ECOSYSTEM MAINTENANCE

However you choose to bring water into the landscape, it is important to remember that ponds, streams, and even simple birdbaths all require regular maintenance. Not

only are water features complete ecosystems in their own right, but they also get cluttered with leaf litter, attract creatures you may not have intended to host, and tend to grow algae and other greenery above and beyond the water lilies and irises you so carefully planted. Whatever balance you achieve upon installation will take regular adjustments and regulations to maintain. And if you live in an area with a real winter, you will have to take special care of any introduced wildlife, such as fish, and remove pumps and bring fountains or other sculpture inside (depending on what they're made of) so they don't freeze and crack.

In spite of—or perhaps because of—the demands of water features, their benefits are many. Once the work is done, nothing is quite so soothing to the soul as the sight and sound of an artful composition of stone, water, and plants.

Flat, man-made stepping stones interspersed with natural boulders create an interplay of textures within the shifting surface of water.

A long, narrow trough, ringed with stones, creates a linear statement of serenity in a garden protected by old barn walls.

STARTING WITH **A SINGLE TREE**

"IT WAS EXTREMELY GRIM," says Greg Trutza, owner of New Directions in Landscape Architecture, of his first look at this site adjacent to the Sonoran desert near Phoenix, Arizona. "They built this elaborate town home and muscled it into a very small lot, so the backyard was cut into a stony, hard hillside with a water canal running behind it. People could walk along the canal and look over the walls; there was a major highway artery nearby; and this was just a concrete yard with a kidney-shaped pool and an archaic barbecue. Plus the house had water seeping into it." Before Trutza could begin to plan the space, he had to demolish everything and call in civil engineers to create an elaborate drainage system to get water away from the house. The only thing he retained from the original installation was a solitary ficus tree and a few cacti in a far corner.

Once the area was cleared, Trutza could begin thinking about what he was going to make of this blank slate, 30 to 50 feet (9.3 m × 15.4 m) deep and 90 feet (27.4 m) long. Fortunately, he notes, the owners are well traveled, well educated, with an open attitude, and a "deep appreciation" of both Japanese aesthetics and the native desert landscape in which they live. "The house is done in a Frank Lloyd Wright style" notes Trutza, "a contemporary home with wonderful, strong, angular themes, so I felt a modern Zen approach would work."

ESCAPING THE SPIRITS

To achieve this desert-influenced, up-to-date Asian vision, Trutza incorporated several elevations and lots of angles, which allowed him to bring in multiple water elements as well as an important spiritual component. "I wanted a rectilinear format," he says, "so the space could capture

An artful combination of small terraces, stone platforms, shallow pools, and planters creates a contemplative landscape with enough room for small gatherings, wandering, wading, and drifting on a floating raft.

elements such as a spirit path, which is a philosophy employed in Asian gardens to keep spirits from pursuing you. Zigzags and breaks in the linear flow foil the spirits and keep them from charging through the landscape." By creating terraces, Trutza not only gave the space dimension, interest, and depth but also made possible a waterfall. Steps through the pond's levels gently encourage visitors to meander and view the landscape from a variety of vantage points. While Trutza characterizes the ponds as "an interconnected, chlorinated wading pool," he did make the larger pond big and deep enough to float a raft and catch the sun. The series of smaller sitting areas give the owners—who do not have children and do not entertain extensively—peaceful places for reading, contemplation, and small gatherings. "It's an adult yard," Trutza says.

Once the structure was in place, Trutza added stonework and plantings that take their aesthetic lead from the

desert surroundings. The house is flanked by the drama of the 2,608-foot (792 m) Piestewa Peak, so Trutza drew on the colors and textures of a variety of local rocks. "They wanted rugged stones in there," he says, "so we used native stone with rich colors—taupes, grays, and blacks, plus strong amounts of ocher and rust."

In keeping with the southwestern theme, the waterfall is made from a Mexican stone called Pinon Adoquin and the river rocks that line the pools are Mexican beach pebbles. "They're what nature does," Trutza points out, "and they're fabulous as a ground cover. The water and the black rocks give the whole place an air of depth and mystery." To reflect the owners' international sensibility, the red wall is made with a clay plaster from Italy that has

▶ Black round stones from Mexico line the pool bottoms, while a series of zigzags in the hardscape encourages meandering—and, according to Asian tradition, foils negative spirits bent on pursuit.

A rosy wall made with an Italian pigmented clay enlivens a corner with color. Water trickles from a hand-carved scupper set in the wall into a basin.

"a smooth, buttery texture that's a great contrast with the other stonework," he says. The triangular sculptures are chiseled granite imported from Japan; and, more prosaically, the pavers are Tioga, commonly known as bluestone, from New York State. "This kind of stone is a real rarity in this part of the world," Trutza notes. "The pavers are predominantly gray with gold tones or olive streaks. Because of the intense light here, I need to use dark surfaces, or otherwise it gets washed out."

FLOATING FIREPIT

Trutza added the element of fire to his stone and water creation with a firepit that appears to be on its own, floating island. "It's isolated by water and soil," he notes, "and you have to go over the bridge from one direction, you have to cross over, so it's a destination in its own right."

Finally, Trutza added plants. "One of the parameters of the job was that it had to be a xeriscape," he says. "It's hard to grow anything in all that rock, so we had to create a raised planter. All the plants require low levels of water and are architectural pieces in their own right." Cacti,

palms, and spiked aloes predominate, softened here and there with a deep purple or magenta spray of flowers. "You think a swimming pool will soften the hardscape," Trutza points out, "but it's still hardscape, so you have to have enough plant material to soften all that." He also added acacia trees, Australian natives whose white trunks provide vertical interest and, in a decade or so, will provide the garden with welcome shade. "While I had sketched this out, of course," Trutza says, "it's always thrilling and pleasing to see it manifest in real form. There's a wonderful balance of soft and hard elements."

▶ A firepit that appears to float atop a pedestal becomes a destination in itself and brings the important element of fire to balance the stone, water, and plants.

Buff-colored stones reflect the desert landscape, while plants with strong forms and upright habits bring a touch of color and vertical structure to the horizontal lines of the stonework.

A POOL FOR ALL SEASONS

IT ALL BEGAN WITH landscape lighting. "This client had a significant landscape he'd already done," recalls landscape architect Bob Hursthouse. "He called me in simply to look at landscape lighting because he was really proud of his plantings and wanted to show them off." Sitting at the kitchen table, looking out over a large deck that featured a big railing, an oversized fiberglass hot tub, and a hedge, Hursthouse pointed out the railing was not required by code and the contraption obscured the view

to the garden. "Within twelve hours of talking to me, he took out his hammer and knocked down the railing and cut down the hedge," Hursthouse says, chuckling. Suddenly, Hursthouse had a more interesting landscape project to contend with.

The client is also an avid outdoorsman who loves natural materials, especially water moving over rocks that remind him of the beloved trout streams in which he's fished. As they talked about the hot tub and other options

▼ A large deck surrounded by a railing and a hedge once obstructed this open view of the homeowner's extensive gardens. A project that began with a request for landscape lighting became both more extensive and more interesting once the railings were knocked down and the hedge was cut away.

▶ The waterfall creates a thunderous, natural sound as it cascades from a spa to a basin and then over an 8-foot (2.4 m) ledge reminiscent of the owner's beloved trout streams.

for the ½-acre (0.2 hectare) suburban Chicago lot, they decided to create an organic-shaped pool with two spas. One is close to the house, easily accessed at any time of year, while the other is on the far side of the pool. All the elements come together with stonework and a waterfall that completes the naturalistic vignette. According to Hursthouse, "The stonework brings the organic form of the pool forward and makes it look like the water could be flowing away from you. We wanted to create a significant flow of water, a thunderous flow. So we used the spa, which is raised 3 feet (1 m) away from the pool, as the headwaters, if you will, for the stream." The circulating water starts in the hot tub, falls into a basin, then spills over the 8-foot (2.4 m) waterfall into the pool. "We really wanted it to feel like a rock bluff and outcropping," he continues.

PUSH-BUTTON WATERFALL

Even if the hot tub is not being used, the water can still be circulated over the waterfall. A remote device controls a valve and heater that, in turn, control the water flow. "When you want to go in the hot tub, you press a button, and it takes about twenty minutes to heat up," explains Hursthouse. "Then, when you're done with the spa, you can push the button that changes the flow so the water from the pool goes into the spa and causes the waterfall to run even bigger."

The naturalized setting is emphasized with a series of important details. While the bluestone patios are dry laid—except right at the edge of the pool, where the additional strength of concrete is required—the Pennsylvania fieldstone walls are set with deep-raked mortar

The stonework, pool, waterfall, and plantings are designed to reflect the contours and serenity of more naturally wild places. Paths lead to secluded sitting areas and two spas.

joints that hide the concrete. The stonework is extended in a number of areas right to the floor of the pool so stone is visible through the water. A stone ledge where swimmers can take a break and sit runs a few feet below the water line on one side. A series of raised stone planters encircles the pool, "creating the illusion that the pool is flowing between two rock bluffs," Hursthouse points out. At the far end of the pool, two stone swim-outs about 18 inches (46 cm) deep obviate the need for chrome pool ladders. Paths meander among the plantings, leading to a small sunning patio with a few lounge chairs and around the back to the spa hot tub and another small patio with a firepit.

"The best thing about this pool is that it looks great twelve months a year," Hursthouse feels. "So many pools are great when you're in them but are not much to look at otherwise." The homeowner maintains a low pool temperature during spring and fall so he can keep the water flowing, and heats it to full swim temperature during the summer. "Even in dead of winter," Hursthouse says, "you have the snow on the stone and branches, and your first reaction is, 'This is a pool?'"

A stone ledge for resting was installed just below the surface of the water near the waterfall, while swim-outs at the far end of the pool make railings unnecessary. The pool was constructed to look like a pond carved out of naturally occurring rock ledges.

WEEPING **WALL**

WHEN THE PARTNERS of biota, A Landscape Design + Build Firm in Minneapolis, Minnesota, were given the job of landscaping the property of a new home for an active family that entertained regularly, they had a complex set of issues to deal with. According to Steve Modrow, "The front of the house is a 2005 version of a Victorian home. We tried to bring a modern aesthetic to that architecture and make it relevant to today's lifestyle." This meant making it low maintenance, improving flow from interior to exterior spaces, enhancing entertaining opportunities, adding a croquet lawn, ensuring whatever was done would look interesting from the second-story deck and third-story windows, creating privacy from a bike bath that runs between the yard and the lake, and preserving the "views they paid for," according to Modrow.

The designers knew they needed a retaining wall between the driveway and the backyard. This feature was critical to keeping the view from the driveway open toward the lake and necessary to establishing a sense of closure and privacy. However, Modrow and partner Jim

A vertical and invisible pondlike construction circulates water from a catch basin at the bottom, sends it up behind the wall, and then allows it to seep over the stonework, creating beautiful, subtle effects as the water trickles over the rocks.

Saybolt brought interesting and inventive dimensions to what could have been a straightforward masonry project. They chose Chilton stone, a material native to the area that reflects nearby limestone bluffs. "This wall is a way to bring the native landscape into the yard without being too literal," Modrow explains. Then, to add to the wow factor of the project, the partners developed a way to build a low-maintenance water feature as part of the wall; water seeps from behind the wall and trickles gently over the vertical surface.

TRADE SECRETS

While they're reluctant to divulge all the secrets to the weeping wall construction, Saybolt will say they used pond-building techniques, including a lined catch basin at the bottom that runs laterally to a reservoir. From there, water is brought up to a perforated pipe behind the wall that releases water over the stones. To increase the splash-ing sounds, they let some stones jut forward to create miniwaterfalls. The whole arrangement is tied into the irrigation system and remote controlled for ease of use. Lights intensify the drama at night, and when the water isn't running, the homeowners festoon the ledges with tea lights or small flower arrangements. Even without adorn-ment, "the weathered stone looks simply gorgeous when it's wet," Saybolt notes.

From the base of this water feature, Saybolt and Modrow built a small patio for intimate gatherings and an adjacent croquet field. This area is connected to an expansive patio that runs along the back of the house and is used for dining with larger groups. "We looked at ways to mediate the large field of pavers without doing the obvious thing of switching up the patterns or colors," Modrow says. Again, an interesting idea, creatively executed, provided the solution. They created a "stone carpet" that reflects the shape of a round dining table the owners intended to

A second-story deck looks over and leads down to an intimate patio that curves along the weeping wall. The formal patch of lawn is a croquet pitch. A public bike path and the lake are just a few feet away.

The smaller and larger patios are connected literally and visually with a variety of paving and natural stone in colors of soft gray and sand with rosy undertones.

use. The "carpet" also gives anyone looking down from the third floor of the house an interesting focal point.

Stone planters, 2 feet (0.5 m) tall, were placed along the edge of the patio to provide privacy from people using the common bike path, just a few feet away, without obscuring the view to the lake. "It's like a doorway onto the lawn so you don't feel totally enclosed," notes Modrow. A final touch was to take the dead space under the deck and turn it into a "secret" room complete with outdoor daybed. Continuity is created by repeating the Chilton stone in places throughout the site.

BUILDING TIPS

Saybolt offers several important construction tips. "Whenever you're working with water and stone, the weathered edge and the naturally occurring rust colors will wear off, so we sealed the limestone wall so the color wouldn't degrade." He cautions to choose products carefully, as "you want to make sure the sealants will not harm plants or water life and are not slippery or toxic." He also suggests avoiding plain sand and mortar when building a patio, especially in a harsh northern climate. "There are interesting products out there that mix polymers with sand and allow it to expand and contract with freeze-and-thaw cycles. You won't track sand inside onto hardwood floors, and it won't chip or crack like concrete would." As in this project, you can also add powdered dyes to the material between the pavers to accentuate the color of the rocks.

As might be expected with this degree of attention to detail, Saybolt says, the landscape in general and the wall in particular "have become quite a conversation piece around the development."

A larger patio includes a "stone carpet" that offers a focal point from windows above as well as a central location for a large dining table. Planters create privacy from the nearby bike path without obstructing views to the lake and mountains beyond.

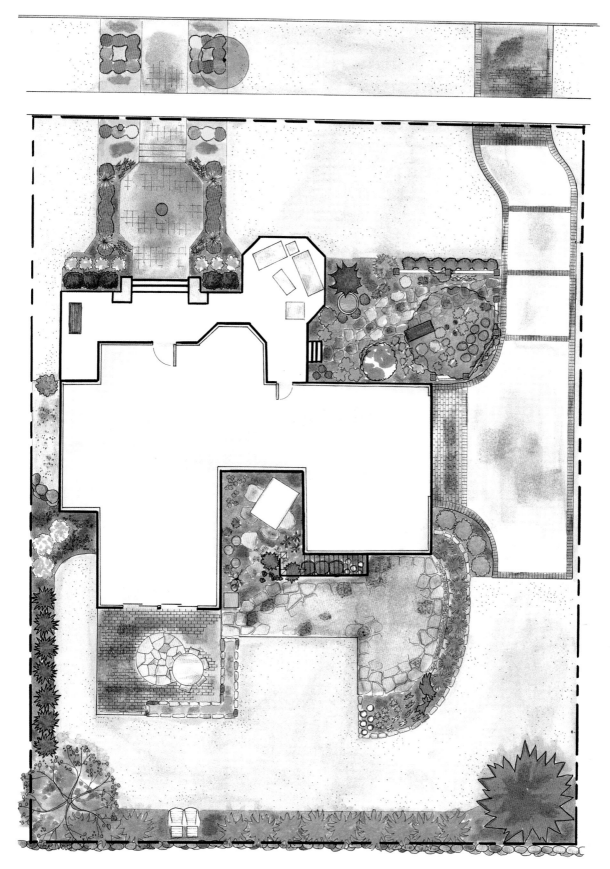

The landscape plan includes extensive gardens and patio spaces at the front of the house and a sheltered room, complete with daybed, which takes advantage of the normally unused space under the deck.

In a plan that was passed from one homeowner to another, a stream flows from the center of three French doors, then wends its way through a wild landscape toward more formal constructions of patios and lawn.

A PARADIGM-BUSTING PLAN

SAM WILLIAMSON CREATED a customized landscape plan for this house in Dover, Massachusetts, but the developer ran out of money and left the building and landscape undone. "There was just hardpan, clay, and subsoil there," recalls Williamson, of Williamson & Associates in Portland, Oregon. However, the developer showed potential buyers the plan and used it to help sell the house. The approach worked; the buyer not only kept the plan as originally conceived but had it quickly implemented. "He took it as whole cloth," Williamson says, "exactly as we'd planned it."

"Normally, landscape design is done in these dissipating rings that radiate from the hard architecture of the house outward to more and more wilderness as you move farther away," Williamson explains. "I was trying to flip this paradigm a little here and start with shady, woodsy at the house, with the more formal paved terrace farther away." To this end, Williamson included several key features in the landscape. There is a main courtyard formed and wrapped by the three sides of the house, all of which include many multipaned windows and French doors. Pathways lead from the doors through the courtyard to terraces for sitting and dining and then to the manicured lawn beyond. "We wanted to make this gesture of two limestone paths that run through the French doors toward the distant landscape," he says. Beyond the paved elements, the grand lawn steps down over a low stone curb, broken at regular intervals with square bluestone plinths set with candle-lit lanterns. Of the curb, Williamson says, "It's not a functional thing as much as expressing the radiating energy running out from the garden." Beyond the lawn, the real woods begin, providing a framework for the entire site.

RADIATING OUTWARD

The lush courtyard close to the house was created as "a shady retreat from the big south-facing windows," Williamson notes. The main feature of the space is a stone-edged, lushly planted stream bed that begins as a pool set just outside the middle French door. "The whole thing starts with a circular pond that pours into a small winding stream, which in turn pours into a rectangle at the lower of the ponds. Then there is an arc at the edge of terrace, and then the arc of patios, and the curb with the lanterns on them. It's all a reference to these radiating views that move outward and gesture to the larger landscape around it."

The first small pond is only about 18 inches (46 cm) in diameter and features a waterfall that drops into a runnel. "I wanted to create the feeling of motion through water that seems to be running out toward the horizon,"

The stream starts with a small pool and waterfall and then flows among rocks, birch trees, and brightly flowering plants. The sound of falling water—the first of several landscape elements—and the naturalized plantings invite visitors to step outside.

he explains. "The runnel is about 12 inches (30.5 cm) wide and 20 feet (6 m) long, and it curves as if it were trying to go around the two birch trees." The stream is "set up like a long, narrow pond," with a recirculating pump. In addition to the birch trees, the stream bed is planted with a Japanese maple, low-growing thymes, mosses, irises, and aquatic plants. "The flower colors are yellow and orange, as it was meant to be sunny and brightly colorful," Williamson says.

COMPLEMENTARY PATTERNS

The site features a variety of stones set in several patterns. "The lighter limestone paths are the bright lines that run through the garden," he points out. "They increase the longitudinal aspect and express these long views from the house out to the horizon. We used cut stones to get the joints tight." The pattern of the stones was borrrowed from a project done in France by the legendary Gertrude Jekyll and Edwin Lutyens. "The squares and rectangles, of course, form an old and common pattern," Williamson says, "But Jekyll and Lutyens added an occasional diagonal joint imi-

A shaded dining area is set just around the corner from the stream. Pavers in complementary colors connect the elements of the landscape, even as each is marked by a slightly different pattern of stones and set with gaps of varying width.

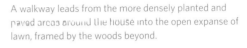

A walkway leads from the more densely planted and paved areas around the house into the open expanse of lawn, framed by the woods beyond.

tating repairs made to the occasional broken stones, which adds a certain amount of visual interest. I've always wanted to use this pattern, and here was my chance."

Williamson also created a sitting area from which to view the stream, and, around the corner, a dining area made of regular bluestone and banded with an edge of lilac bluestone. "The other thing I was playing with in this project," he notes, "is using all kinds of stones together. I've always noticed that if you look at a collection of tile samples, the color range is very wide. But with stone, the colors tend to hang together better than you might think. So I was playing with all kinds of stone to see if it might

work; there's bluestone, lilac bluestone, limestone, and local, native fieldstone."

While the homeowner who finally saw this job to completion likes it best as a place to stroll in the evening, especially by moonlight, Williamson is most intrigued with the formal aspects of the plan, even as they result in a naturalized setting. "I like the clarity of the diagram," he says. "It's these two lines that run out from the house and are overlaid with this circle of water; then these parallels are intersected with an arc that gets more and more open as it radiates outward. It's all about expressing the connection of the house and the overall landscape."

A curving stone curb in the middle of the lawn is set with lanterns on plinths and expresses the "radiating energy running out from the garden."

BRIDGE BETWEEN TWO PATIOS

WHEN KATHY SWEHLA of Land Expressions in Mead, Washington, was first contacted about this project, she almost turned it down. The owners of a house in Spokane simply wanted a grape arbor in an area of native plants. However, when she sat down with them, she uncovered some much bigger ideas that started with a very big rock.

"The property had what's called a haystack rock," she says. "It's lava flow that was once covered with earth. When the earth wore away, this is what's left behind." In this case, the haystack rock was 30 feet (9 m) high, next to a cliff. "The husband always thought it would be cool to have a waterfall coming off that rock, and he wanted a better front yard," Swehla explains, "So I envisioned a small, natural-looking pond with a little bridge over it leading to the front door. That was the original idea." But as the project was being installed, at every step of the way the owners began to see what was possible and asked for more.

Because the yard is long and narrow, with only one access point—a ramp 65 feet (20 m) long and 8 feet (2.4

▶ What was once a small lawn and a straight brick porch accessed by a concrete ramp is now a tropical lagoon complete with pool, hot tub, and cascading waterfall.

▶ Water is piped up behind a haystack rock, a 30-foot (9 m) outcropping of basalt left in a hillside after erosion removed the surrounding earth. The water falls into a stream bed made from rocks gathered on site and then feeds into the pool.

m) wide—the project started at the far side of the lot, with the haystack rock. The rock couldn't be drilled, so Swehla's team ran a pipe up the back, hiding it among the plants, and then cascaded water down the front of the stone into a 15-foot (4.6 m) stream feeding what was to be a small pond. The owners loved this effect so much they asked for a hot tub where they could sit and enjoy the view. This necessitated filling in the already excavated pond to gain access to the hot tub site at the far corner of the house. "After they had the hot tub," Swehla recalls, "they thought it would be fun to be able to take a dip in cool water," which meant expanding and deepening the pond. "Then they decided they didn't want it too cool, so a heater was added. By the time it was done, the design had gone from a 6-foot (2 m) bridge to a 20-foot (6 m) span over the pool."

MAKE IT SPARKLE

Other additions were made as well. The original house had a straight front porch made of brick tile. By curving the wall of the pool, they were able to create a larger, more organic and inviting porch of random-sized, quartzite stone from Idaho. "It has lots of mica in it, so it's sparkly," notes Swehla. The quartzite is grout-set on concrete and is also used to create planters that are integral to the patio. The bridge, which is built on buttresses set into the ground, is made of poured concrete with beach glass set in the surface. "The beach glass is tossed by hand into random curves," Swehla says. "It's gold and red and brown

▶ An informal bistro area was carved out of the hillside and made accessible with sand-set quartzite and steps of Iron Mountain stone. Plants grow freely among the basalt boulders found on site.

▼ The formal patio with integrated planters next to the house is made of quartzite rock grout-set on concrete; the bridge is concrete with golden beach glass set into the surface.

and catches the sun quite beautifully." The bridge also led to a path up the hillside across from the pool. "The owners loved the area so much, they asked if there was a way to create more space by making a landing of some kind," Swehla says. So she carved out a bistro sitting area from the slope by building small walls from native basalt rock. Iron Mountain stone was used to create natural-looking steps.

The overall plan became a series of successive styles worked together in layers. "Up near the house, we went with a formal look and traditional plantings," Swehla notes. "Then, as we moved up the hill and away from the house, we created a more informal sitting area and more native plantings." The result is "an interesting mix of tropical plantings, a formal European feel to the house and patios, and a transition into a native forest."

As she looks back on the project now, Swehla feels it is a great example of integrating a house into the larger landscape. "This is something people often overlook—the opportunities to transition from the architecture of the house and sitting areas, such as a deck, to more naturalized outdoor sitting areas in the garden," she says. "Instead of having the house and deck be an island in a landscape, use the components to create transition and places where you can sit and look back at the house rather than always looking outward. I encourage homeowners to walk their space, get out a lawn chair, sit in various areas, and see what it feels like to be there."

The formality of the materials and colors closest to the house is relieved by increasingly casual plantings, stonework, and furniture on the hillside.

Asian Influences

Professionally designed Japanese and Asian-influenced landscapes incorporate centuries of tradition that reflect careful planning and structured restraint to create a pervasive feeling of serenity and peacefulness. However, similar results can be achieved in the home landscape by considering a few critical elements.

• **Sanctuary:** Asian gardens are created for reflection, not for entertaining or playing sports. Decisions about how to contour the land and the plants or other elements to include are made to encourage thinking about nature and the lessons she has to teach.

• **Natural elements:** To represent balance, the critical elements of water, fire, stone, and plants should all be included in some way. Water could appear in a shallow bowl; fire as a lantern; stones on pathways or as sculptural elements.

• **Asymmetry:** The inherent asymmetry of nature is celebrated even as it is controlled. Groupings of plants and stones are made in odd numbers. Paths turn, twist, or zigzag to direct the gaze to different views. Formal lines and geometric compositions are eschewed.

• **Borrowed landscape:** Asian gardens often take advantage of distant landscape elements. Trees may be planted to frame a miles-away mountaintop. Rocks may be arranged to reflect the shape of much larger hillsides. This gives the visitor a sense of connectedness and makes compact spaces seem larger.

Texture and form are prized over color in Asian gardens. Here, the round basin is accented by the smooth river rocks and the vertical forms of the arching grasses. Water, even in this simple expression, is an important element that enhances peaceful contemplation.

Serenity is achieved by the subtle layering of simple forms and patterns. The strong lines of the paved walkway are balanced by the organically shaped bed in the distance, the rounded forms of carefully placed rocks, the upright lantern, and the complementary colored gravel, delicately raked into graceful patterns.

The combination of a high degree of control along with an appreciation for organic forms is fully realized in this sculptural creation that uses three kinds of rocks in an evocative, sinewy shape.

• **Minimalism:** Asian gardens focus on simplicity of texture and pattern. Beds may be filled with raked gravel, encouraging contemplation of the subtle motif. Water does not spout from a fountain but rather trickles down a streambed or drips from a cut piece of bamboo, connecting ears and eyes to the beauty of the natural world. Plants are chosen for their sculptural form more than their blooms. A few elements, artfully arranged, are all that is required to create a garden that is beautiful, low maintenance, and interesting to view in all seasons.

Chapter 4

STONE AND PLANTS

HARDSCAPES OF STONE WALLS, patios, and walks are always improved by the softening influence of plants. There is something inherently balanced and pleasing about the sight of stems arching over a boulder, moss creeping around a stone, a bright colored bloom against the mottled gray of a wall. While the iconic image of an ancient stone wall fronted by densely planted clusters of perennials is familiar to every garden enthusiast, this is only one—and a high-maintenance one, at that—of many effective ways to combine stones and plants.

The tumbling boulders of a classic New England piled farmhouse wall are enlivened by the bright blooms of a casual, low-maintenance perennial border featuring rugged daylilies and phlox.

A rooftop garden in Australia is bisected with granite slabs that attract the eye with their undulating outline. They also serve to contain the thin layer of soil necessary for these low-growing plants.

Along this inviting stone path, roses in many colors bloom over an underplanting of annuals, while vertical interest is created with a clematis vine climbing a lamppost.

The edges of a large patio can be decorated with architecturally-inspired planters filled with easily maintained, ever-blooming, brightly colored annuals and cascading vines. If you have a rock wall in a moist, shady location, you can adorn the base with small spring bulbs like snowdrops and crocus as well as woodland plants like hostas, whose large and variegated foliage is a perfect foil for the stones. For your informal patio or walkway, tuck creeping thyme, sedum, or any of a wide variety of other "step-able," ground-hugging plants into gaps between the stones, and enjoy the contrast of clusters of tiny bright blooms against sober gray. Create beds alongside your pavers, fill them with bold sweeps of low-maintenance ornamentals such as grasses or compact shrubs, and make a statement of modern minimalism. Herbs are an especially appropriate accompaniment to stonework, as most of them thrive in the well-drained, warm soils that usually exist alongside the walls. They offer delicious and festive additions to your outdoor cooking adventures as well.

SHADE AND IRRIGATION

Stonework also benefits from the addition of trees; the vertical element draws the eye upward and creates welcome shade on heat-soaked stones. The white, peeling bark of a cluster of fast-growing birch trees provides textural interest and the comforting sound of a breeze rustling the leaves while you're sipping coffee on your bluestone patio. Lilac bushes fill the air with welcome perfume as you're feeding the fish in your stone-edged pond. A lemon tree grants easy access to garnish for drinks or grilled fish when you're entertaining guests al fresco.

If you plan carefully, you can also install irrigation systems at the same time you're installing your stonework. Soaker hoses and drip systems are not only unobtrusive but also waste less water by putting moisture right where it's needed most. Not only can they be set into seasonal planters, which tend to dry out quickly, but many systems can easily be programmed and remote controlled so your blooms will stay in peak condition even when you're out of town.

A GARDEN PHOTOGRAPHER'S GARDEN

CLIVE NICHOLS, a leading garden photographer in England, began with an old barn and a forsaken cow yard. "It was just an abandoned dirt yard," Nichols recalls. "You couldn't put a shovel in it. And the walls were covered with corrugated iron sheets for a roof." And yet, from this inauspicious space of approximately 30 by 30 yards (27.4 × 27.4 m), he has created a home, a place of work, and a contemplative courtyard garden.

It was a process both organic and backbreaking. "I just did it by eye," Nichols says. "I didn't plan it out. I just wanted it to be very natural and use only natural materials. I didn't want anything modern in there." He also did it by muscle, handpicking each and every rock in the garden from what he found both on site and at a local quarry.

▼ Purples and yellows punctuate a field of blond stones and gravel to create a contemplative courtyard garden alongside an old barn that was turned into a house. The garden was designed to maximize photographic opportunities.

▶ The garden began as nothing more than an abandoned cow yard. An opening in an existing wall leads to a lawn where the children play and an area around the corner where the family dines.

"The edging rocks came literally out of the ground," he notes. "They're quite lovely, as they have a lot of shells and fossils in them." The stone seats were also picked out individually, but because they had been machine cut, Nichols had them "dragged around the quarry to rough them up." The seats were brought into the site by forklift and then nudged about with heavy iron rods to finalize placement. "They are the main part of the garden," Nichols says. "They hold it all together."

He also banged up some slices of stone to use as pavers that transition from the inside to outdoors. "I wanted to walk out of the house onto a massive pavement of huge rocks drifting away from the door, but it was too expensive," he says, "so we got slices and had them rough up the edges to give them a bashed-up look like the barn, so it's not too perfect."

STRAW WALL

To intensify the enclosed feeling of the garden, Nichols built one wall to complement the existing ones. Using 100 bales of straw, he mocked up where the wall was to go and how high it should be. "People thought we were nuts," he laughs, "but it turned out perfect because the bales were the same thickness as the wall. Afterwards, the straw went to bedding for the horses." The finished wall includes an opening that allows access "so you're enclosed but you don't feel like you're in prison," Nichols explains, "plus it makes lovely views through the gaps into the garden."

The garden beds themselves were carved out of the hardpan, which was loosened with the addition of many tons of gravel and compost. Nichols chose plants of only a few colors: an occasional birch tree, purple salvias and sage, and a yellow grass. "The salvias smell when you brush against them, the birch has pink fleshy tones, and the wispy grass is like blonde hair, so it's a great foil for other things," Nichols notes. While many plants are contained behind rock borders or in planters, others, like the grasses, are free to seed themselves wherever they find a suitable growing spot. "I like the idea of sitting on the seat with all this stuff foaming around," he says.

◀ A few carefully chosen and well-placed elements create visual interest; a driftwood spire, a shallow water basin that attracts birds and reflects the sky, and an inviting purple cushion accent the predominantly blonde landscape.

Nichols brought in just a few other elements for contrasting forms and continued visual interest. There is a 20-foot (6 m) piece of driftwood rising sculpturally from the back of one bed, its gray pallor dramatic against the stone walls. A shallow bowl is set into the ground in the sitting area as a gazing pool "so you can see the sky reflected in it, and the birds come to it." In keeping with the "bashed-up" theme, the natural freeze-and-thaw cycle has cracked and aged the bowl, "but it did it in a very lovely way, actually," Nichols says. Punctuation comes in the form of several bronze-plated planters that spread seasonal blooms against their soothing patina.

A wall was mocked up with straw bales and then constructed of complementary stone to increase the sense of privacy—but with an open gate to maintain a sense of flow and intrigue about what lies on either side.

RUSTIC ZEN

While the garden is too exposed to wind and weather to make a suitable eating area—another courtyard on a different side of the barn-cum-house is where meals are served al fresco—this area is used for serving drinks, relaxing, gardening, and contemplation. "It's kind of circular and enclosed and bowl-like," Nichols explains, "so you feel quite safe in there. We call it 'rustic Zen' because it's got a lot of spirit to it; it's a very spiritual place with lovely views."

The site is located 20 miles (32 km) north of Oxford in Banbury, England. The stone is known locally as ironstone, for the bit of iron oxide that highlights the golden hue. Carrying this sun-burnished color throughout, Nichols compacted the already leaden clay soil and brought in gravel to create a foundational stone carpeting in the courtyard. "The stone is the most pleasing thing because when the sun is on it, you get this rich honey color. And it changes; sometimes it looks like treacle, other times like sand. Even in the winter it can look lovely," he says. Then, after a pause, "It can also look bloody awful, especially when you have a moody sky, but all gardens are like that. It is essentially a photographer's garden," he adds. "I designed it so I could photograph it."

▶ Stones for seats were chosen at a local quarry and then dragged around by machinery to soften the cut edges and achieve a carefully orchestrated "bashed-up" look. Some plants are contained in beds and planters; others are left to seed themselves at will.

All the stones in the yard were individually chosen and placed. These edging stones were found on site. Many contain fossils.

Bluestone pavers have been mixed with more naturally shaped stones, as well as creeping plants in a range of colors and textures, to create a pattern to walk through or view from above.

PEBBLES, ROCKS, AND BLUESTONE

THE OWNERS OF this oddly shaped and sloping site in the hills west of Portland, Oregon, were avid vegetable gardeners. Now in their 80s, "it was getting to be too much to pull out the rototiller every year," said Sam Williamson of Samuel H. Williamson & Associates in Portland, Oregon. So they requested an Asian-inspired, low-maintenance garden to replace the tomato, pepper, and pea plants. "What I did instead," said Williamson, "was my take on American gardens from the 1950s that were supposedly Asian-inspired, and then I made it more contemporary."

The house and garden area have been carved out of a hill. The house is a single story in the front and two stories in the back, with a "daylight basement" that opens out onto the 40-foot-by-40-foot (12.2 × 12.2 m) shelf that is the garden. This setting created both challenges and opportunities. "We wanted to create a garden that was an

A compact garden space becomes an interesting array of garden rooms with the introduction of pathways and a variety of textures in plants and stone.

interesting pattern to look down on from the upper floor of the house, and also wanted to create a lot of variety in a very tight space," Williamson explains. He used two techniques to achieve these goals and make the space feel more expansive: introducing a series of pathways and using a wide variety of textures in both stone and plant material.

"One of the first ideas I had was to create a walk-through ground cover," Williamson recalls. "And this is an abstraction of an authentic Japanese garden detail, where you have bridges that zigzag across water features. The idea is that ghosts travel in a straight line, and as they follow you, they'll fall in the water and drown. So when you get to the end of the bridge, you'll feel more peaceful." Williamson also created a separate pedestrian path with a row of cedars on one side and junipers along the other. "I wanted the views to keep changing," he notes. "You start on the upper deck with expansive views of the Oregon coast range, and then as you descend, you get into a more closed-in world, with teasing glimpses into the garden. It's about adding some feeling of progression, rather than seeing the whole thing from the start."

TEXTURE AND COMPLEXITY

At the furthest end of the walk is a garden room planted with a vine maple grove among bluestone and pebbles. "It's meant to feel like a destination, but also like a terrace and a pathway you pass through, as well as a decorative abstraction that you can see from above," he says. This sense of passing from one place to another and seeing a plethora of textures, including bluestone pavers cut in several proportions, Montana moss stone, Mexican beach pebbles, and gravel is also designed to increase the feeling of expansiveness. "Sometimes, to make a small space seem bigger, people tear down walls," Williamson notes. "But if you put up a wall, and create complexity, that makes a space seem bigger, too."

The textural complexity is extended to the plant choices. Irish moss, creeping thyme, blue star creeper, ferns, and brass buttons grow among the stones. Japanese kerria, vine maples, cedars, and junipers add vertical interest while bright flowers are used as accents. "It's rich, but not a wild mix," Williamson notes, "and we wanted to make it feel a bit like the Pacific Northwest woods by, for instance, adding in some ferns." He also added an island

The subdued and cohesive palette of blues, grays, and browns inherent in stone of almost any kind provides a soothing backdrop for plants as well as fallen leaves.

A vine maple grove is planted among bluestone and Mexican river rocks to offer visitors a place to linger or pass through on their way to other parts of the garden.

of boulders set amongst the plants to appear as a single stone outcropping.

When choosing plants to place among stones, Williamson offers a few guidelines. "One is that you have to think about the heat that the stones create. Pieces of stone are big heat sinks and some plants really like it, while others hate it," he says. "You need to think about whether you want the ground cover to creep out over the top or to sit neatly along the edge of the stone, because if you choose the wrong one, you end up with a maintenance issue." Color also plays a part. "Stone has a really restricted palette compared to plants," Williamson points out. "For example, bluestone is blue, but not as blue as a blue flower. The color palette of stones hangs together regardless of what kind of stone it is, so I think of stone as a neutral backdrop and then accent around it with plants."

GARDENS FRONT AND CENTER

"THEY WANTED A PLACE to park in the front yard that looked like it was a pedestrian or people space, not a car-parking space," says Keith Wagner, a landscape architect based in Burlington, Vermont, of the design for a ½-acre (0.2 hectare) site in the historic garden district of Cambridge, Massachusetts. "Plus, she was from Wichita Falls, Texas, and wanted to pick up some colors from that part of the world." Wagner also wove in his own historic and personal design sensibilities to create a "contempo-

rary interpretation of the garden traditions of western Europe while integrating the client's own eclectic style." And he threw in some North Texas farming references for good measure.

The result is a series of "flexible garden rooms that explore the relationship between interior and exterior spaces." The "rooms" include an entry court with a terrace and garden, a two-car off-street parking area, spillover parking space in the front yard, a private terrace for a spa,

The front yard of this home becomes a multiuse space for gardening, parking, sitting, and socializing. The low stone wall marks the property boundary while allowing for interaction with passersby.

rear, winter, and cutting gardens, and a children's play area. Wagner also integrated an existing wood deck and pergola with the overall plan.

The entry garden was the most challenging space to work with. "We wanted to create a sense of depth and scale along the street frontage as well as provide an elegant welcome," Wagner says. After studying the geology of the owner's childhood landscape—and discussing it with an employee who just happened to be from the same part of the world—Wagner laid out the area in "alternating bands of stonework and gardens, like crop plantings, an abstraction of agricultural rows." Using buffs, tans, and other southwestern-inspired colors, they built a low wall along the sidewalk that "defines the public space as separate from the semiprivate front yard." They also put in a larger area of stone patio in warm reddish tones where a car can be parked without blocking anyone in the driveway: an essential pre-dawn getaway location for the surgeon in the family. And for those times when the space is car-free, the area is scaled to be inviting and accessible to human traffic as well. The walls are wet laid for strength, while the pavement is dry laid so it can move as weather and weight require. The parking area is set with sturdy stones, 3 inches (7.6 cm) thick, for extra stability.

A SERIES OF SANCTUARIES

The entry garden area as a whole is "bisected by an inviting 'carpet runner' composed of a rich, warm pattern of natural stone." A Euro/Colonial touch is created with the balustrades across the front entryway, which hearken simultaneously to an Italian villa and a New England front porch. Privacy and warmth are enhanced with a series of large planters bursting with both perennials and annuals, a technique that makes garden maintenance a bit simpler. Beds are filled with easy-care grasses, herbs, and low-growing shrubs, while the planters can be changed out for ongoing pops of color.

The walls and stonework continue around and behind the house, making more rooms and sanctuaries as they go. "There's a series of walls along the side of the house," Wagner explains. "The first hides the bulkhead to the basement, the second wall steps up to a terrace that provides access to a side door and mud room, and behind the third wall is a hot tub. We're using walls to define space and create privacy." In the backyard, another series of low fieldstone walls forms terraced planting beds, a children's play area, and a level lawn. The existing deck was wrapped with a stone wall so it "didn't look so deck-y. There's nothing worse than looking under a deck," Wagner observes.

The other existing element the landscape designers had to contend with is the strong, traditional Colonial design of the house itself. Wagner made peace with it essentially by leaving it alone. "It was hard to work with,"

A series of walls along the side of the house defines functional spaces and traffic flow while providing privacy for the side entryway and the spa.

The front terrace of this typical New England property features alternating bands of buff-colored hardscape and uniformly planted garden beds, a reference to the agricultural farmlands of the owner's childhood in northern Texas.

he admits. "I hate to say that we almost ignored the house, but because the owner wanted a contemporary garden, it gave us license to look beyond the Colonial architecture and let the house simply be an object within the garden, if you think of the whole site as a garden."

With this new landscaping, the compact site does get much better utilization as a complete garden space. "Previously, they never used the front yard or even went out there," Wagner says. "Now they sit on the front steps, and it becomes a social space in which to chat with neighbors as they walk by. The gardens have really energized the whole front of the house." Much of this energy comes from the cohesive interplay of the many materials and influences. "The whole site is highly textural," Wagner notes. "Textures are part of what make memories for people when they come into a place and then leave."

A large patio is set with 3-inch (7.6 cm)-thick stones so the owners can use it for overflow parking. Wide steps, a grand entrance, and the surrounding plantings keep the scale comfortable for humans as well.

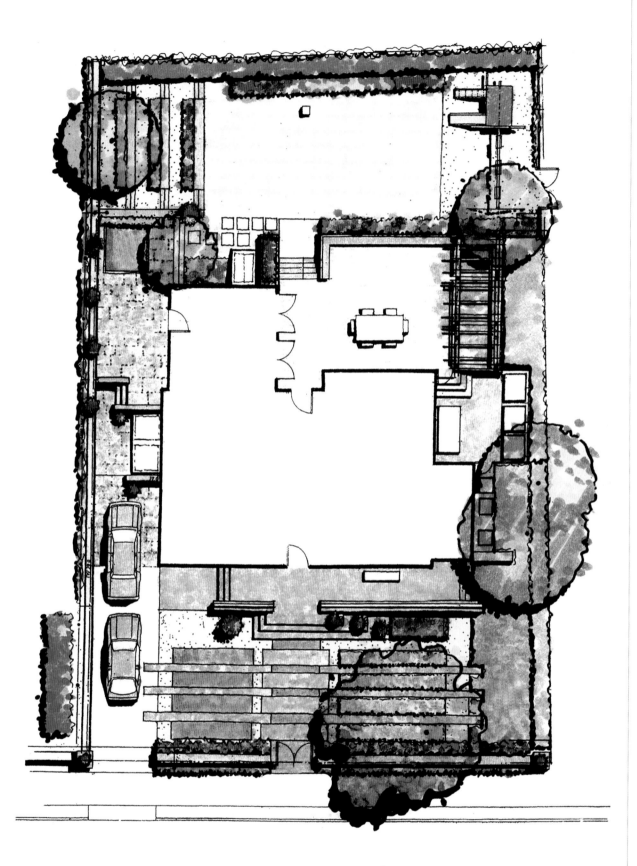

The plan shows how the compact lot was divided into a series of
multifunctional garden "rooms" that increase the property's usability
as well as the quality of life for the owners and their family.

IT'S ALL IN **THEIR NAME**

WITH A LAST NAME LIKE Dejardin, growing up to be a landscape designer might seem inevitable. Then, to carry the theme forward, you might marry a woman named Rose, who would be, appropriately enough, an herbaceous plant specialist and garden designer. Which is exactly what John Dejardin did. Together, over the last twenty-five years, the Dejardins have created Wingwell Garden in Wing, Rutland County, England, the site of their home, business, nursery and, more lately, an annual sculpture show.

The property encompasses 8 acres (3.2 hectares), but the most heavily landscaped area is directly around the home. "The gardens surround the house on three sides," John notes, adding that the nursery is located on the fourth side. "They were designed as a series of rooms that gets larger as you move around the house." These rooms—as well as the flow as you move about the property—are defined, in part, by a series of walls and some inventive stonework.

A series of walls appears to be either diving into or heaved up from the earth. Traditional construction techniques were used, but in a way that expresses a more contemporary theme.

The areas between the walls and in beds throughout the site are filled with exuberant flowering plants, creating an "interplay of texture and drama."

One garden area is notable for a set of walls built so they appear to be heaving out of the ground. Dejardin explains that these walls and the house itself are made of local limestone. "I had this idea of the walls being torn apart and twisting over. It's playing around with the idea of fault lines and natural forces." His brother, a traditional dry stone waller, was enlisted to create these sidelong stone sculptures in a process that was fraught with difficulty. "He did think I was crazy," Dejardin readily confesses. "And everyone was appalled because I made him do it twice. But I'm a great believer in working with the craftsmen," he adds. "They always add something to the process. And it's important that they contribute because they have a great feel for the material. It's not something you should dictate. It was a great collaboration."

COCK AND HEN

The Dejardins used these walls to help create a kitchen-cum-garden-room that works as an intimate sitting area. Because this garden room is below grade, Dejardin created a retaining wall that mirrors the other walls nearby. "It's an abstraction of rock bedding coming out of the ground at 45 degrees," Dejardin says, "which reflects the natural bedding that breaks out. The stone dives right into the paving surface. We're playing with natural rock bedding themes and turning them into something more contemporary," and also nodding to tradition by including upright coping across the top. Dejardin calls this touch "cock and hen" because of its resemblance to the comb that tops a chicken's head.

The heaved stone walls are connected to other stonework and walls throughout the property by a series of culverts broken in such a way as to maximize the coursing, splashing, and sound of water as it moves. "The water erupts out of place," Dejardin explains, "and then it runs down these artificial rills made of concrete with local limestone, which gives it natural qualities. It blends with the limestone and gets iron stains, which give it a nice color." The water flows through and over the rills into a basin, where it is pumped down courses to the main pond. The pond, flanked with stone and plants, has a perfectly round shape that reflects the smaller basin.

A SPACE FOR SCULPTURE

In addition, there is another garden where the Dejardins have held sculpture shows for the last several years. Alongside the traditional stone walls, they built a concrete wall and painted it a deeply saturated red that reflects the color of their front door. "This wall runs straight through the house and out the other side," Dejardin says. "It's part of what creates the event of entering the house." The wall also encloses the appropriately named Wall Garden, which is "a small garden surrounded by the shape of the house." It is here that they host the annual sculpture show. A winged figure, one of their personal pieces of artwork, is outside the walled area and welcomes visitors to the gardens and home.

A garden enclosed by both a traditional wall, complete with coping along the top, as well as a more contemporary concrete wall, painted bright red, provides the setting for an annual sculpture show.

Water appears to erupt directly and naturally from a carefully constructed pile of stone and is moved throughout the property in a series of broken and stepping runnels.

Most of the stonework was created with materials found around the property or repurposed from other stone walls. The beautiful colors inherent in the rocks come from naturally occurring iron. "We get a lot of iron impregnation," Dejardin notes. "We're located on the threshold between pure limestone and ironstone."

The landscape reflects Dejardin's trust in the energy of nature itself. "I always think of the theme of this garden as natural forces you're playing with. The water natu-

rally falls down, and the stones come out of the ground, so we're playing with them erupting out of the ground. There's a whole series of natural forces, and Man interferes with that, and then Nature takes back over." The plantings express this notion as well. "The whole thing about our design is that we're creating niches and habitats and opportunities for things to happen. Things like lichen, mosses, and ferns naturally grow on stone. Thyme and sedum naturally grow on the joints in the stonework."

The water ends up in a formal round pond, a feature whose shape is reflected in the cone-shaped stone element nearby.

The large landscape is filled with a series of smaller, intimate vignettes, such as this feature that combines running water, a variety of stonework, and the cascading blooms of many kinds of plants.

Dejardin characterizes this garden as having "a kind of wild exuberance. It's about the interplay of texture and drama." He creates the situation partially by letting nature have its way. "You just carry on, and the whole thing takes on a life of its own based on the niches and microclimates you create. And, of course, it always changes and evolves around you," he continues. "I'm a great believer that if something is not quite right, it just devolves into something else; it doesn't get torn away."

Rose Dejardin and Keith Wagner on Using Stone and Plants

In this garden, long, angular beds, geometric stones, and the repetition of strong patterns, shapes, colors, and textures yield a composition that is formal without being rigid.

"When you're planting up areas you've artificially created, the most effective way to get it right is to look at landscapes that occur naturally. If you reflect that landscape, the plants will not only look right, but will succeed."

—R.D.

• The starting point would be the microclimate, soil conditions, environment, atmosphere, and feeling you want to create at the site. There is always more than one answer to a problem.

• You want to offset your hardscape with randomly placed plantings that soften it.

• Colors depend on the specific siting. Often, plants suit their environment with their color. For example, Mediterranean plants tend to be silvery and hairy to retain moisture.

• The most common mistake is probably putting plants together that don't like being together. Sometimes plants will be put side by side, and one will be far too vigorous and outstrip the other.

• We like plants that are highly textured so when you compose them with stone, it adds a critical richness.

"Perennial borders and stone walls are a really handsome combination, but I tend to lean toward contemporary themes, so I look at plants as being more about texture."

—K.W.

• I love the uprightness of ornamental grasses as a contrast against the horizontal patterning of stone walls. Another favorite is river birch; the textured bark complements the texture of walls.

• We tend to plant things densely to keep weeds to a minimum; ornamental grasses need to be cut only once, in the spring.

• I use mass plantings and prefer flowers contained in planters that provide a pop of color. Plus, this allows you to make seasonal changes and lowers maintenance. Everyone wants low maintenance, even recognizing there isn't any garden that doesn't require some maintenance.

Chapter 5

STONE CREATIONS

NOT EVERY STONEWORK PROJECT need have a functional requirement. As the following creations show, piles of stone may be artfully arranged into a variety of fanciful, beautiful, symbolic, and meaningful shapes and sizes. There is something about even an inert pile of stones that, as Canadian waller John Shaw-Rimmington suggests, "asks you to get involved." In these projects, not only did the stone itself prove irresistible to the wallers and artisans, but they then went forward to create artifacts that are doubly irresistible to friends, family, neighbors, and the public who have the good fortune to be able to interact with these unique and inspired pieces of artwork.

ARCH

"There's a place near Mount Pleasant in southern Ontario, Canada, where you can see cows grazing; and there are stacks of stones on the crest of a high hill that farmers have collected over the years," John Shaw-Rimmington recalls. "I drove by it many times imagining building an arch just for fun. One day, I saw a farmer there. I figured he'd think I was crazy, but when I told him what I wanted to do, he looked at me and said, 'I've seen you on television.'" The farmer, who had seen Shaw-Rimmington's shows on dry stone walling, gave him permission—with the caveat that he close the gates and promise the cows wouldn't get hurt.

Shaw-Rimmington sent out emails to fellow members of the Dry Stone Wall Association of Canada, calling on wallers and students to get together for a one-day arch-building project. "We got eight or nine people to commit to this one Saturday, and we just went up and did it," he reports. The form for the arch was made from a winnowing machine, giving the entire project "a farm respectability." Loose stones on the ground keep the cows from walking under it. "I wanted to create something that made you think about the past, even though it wasn't a real past," Shaw-Rimmington notes. "You just look at it off in the distance, and it looks like a window from an ancient ruin."

CAIRN

"It was winter, and I was itching to build and get in shape, and there was this lovely pile of stone that had been delivered to my property," says John Shaw-Rimmington as he recalls the genesis of what he calls his Stone-iferous Tree, built in Port Hope, Canada. "It was about five days before Christmas, and I just thought, 'I haven't hugged any stones recently, and I'm going to make a Christmas tree.'" Which was also a kind of protest to his neighbor's over-the-top display of inflatable Santas.

After the season was over, the stone tree came down and the raw materials were repurposed for a client project. But when the next holiday season arrived, he built another Stone-iferous Tree in a different design. Shaw-Rimmington refers to these as "no-brainer" projects. "If you're building without cement," he explains, "then you're committed to having it become more narrow as it goes up. You're reduced to making cheese wedges and Christmas trees."

HELIX

Built as a two-day project for a workshop given by the Dry Stone Wall Association of Canada, this twisted structure was built—and stands—without glue or cement. Designed by John Shaw-Rimmington "to replicate a section of a left-handed double helix Z-DNA molecule," the Rubble Helix stands 10 feet (3 m) tall, twists nearly 90 degrees, and includes six center rungs, each weighing over 300 pounds (136 kg). "The structure can best be interpreted as a whimsical allusion to the primal and essential connection that exists between rocks and people," Shaw-Rimmington says. "All rocks are formed by complex combinations of crystal structures. All crystal configurations grow according to some predetermined pattern based on the certain atom combinations present in the mix. This inorganic patterning may well be the lithological counterpart of organic DNA patterning," he explains. Apparently, the team of wallers would have continued the twist around a full 180 degrees but was constricted by the roof of the building where it was made. Shaw-Rimmington expects an outdoor installation, which may even go 360 degrees, will be attempted in the not-too-distant future.

DOOR TO THE SUN

"The inspiration for the Door to the Sun came about through ancient stone structures around the world used to celebrate changing of the seasons or to measure the winter or summer solstice," says Geoff Duggan, Master Craftsman, dry stone waller, and the landscape planning officer of Mount Annan Botanic Garden in New South Wales, Australia. "The idea came to me," he confesses, "as I was doodling away with my mind elsewhere during a meeting at work. My idea was to have a central sculptural piece that would mark the solstice and the changing of the seasons that plants rely upon for growth." The arch was built with Sydney sandstone using traditional dry stone walling techniques and a "piece of electrical conduit to give me the overall arch shape and to follow as a guide. The center hole was built around a piece of PVC pipe secured on each side for the duration of the construction by a steel pole driven into the ground," Duggan explains. Built first as an exhibition piece, it was then dismantled and rebuilt in the Sydney Botanic Garden, and then again taken down and rebuilt in its current home at the Mount Annan Botanic Garden.

KNOT

The Knot is a focal point for the Wedding Tree Avenue at Mount Annan Botanic Garden in New South Wales, Australia. Geoff Duggan, Master Craftsman, dry stone waller, and the landscape planning officer at the gardens, was asked to "come up with an idea for something to stand out as a feature." He sketched out the Knot—"as in tie the knot"—and, while laid up with an ankle injury, made several scale models from "buckets of gravel and a tube of liquid nails." The Friends of the Royal Botanic Garden, Sydney, provided funding for the project. "All of the stone was brought in from the nearby quarry and hand-split and shaped," Duggan says. "Gravity and friction is what holds it all together, although we did use a little mortar under the caps to help prevent vandalism." The construction took Duggan and three other wallers a month to complete. Promotional materials describe the creation as "a dry stone wall of many stones, built to last, that entwines as it loops over and under itself, symbolizes lasting relationships as each stone represents a memory or emotion, supporting and bonding with each other, in a bid to create permanence."

LABYRINTH

"This is not a maze, and it's not a puzzle," says Ken Mills of this rock creation near Burlington, Vermont. "There's only one way to walk." Part of his extensively landscaped 2-acre (0.8 hectare) garden, this construction is based on a "traditional Celtic labyrinth of seven concentric circles," he explains. "It's generally thought of as a meditative process. As you walk through the labyrinth, it's not obvious how to get to the center, even though there's only one way of walking. As you start getting close to the center, you find yourself closer and then farther away from it. We even tried to find energy lines by dowsing." The labyrinth is about 50 feet (15 m) across and made from hundreds of river rocks that were wheelbarrowed in and set by hand

6 to 8 inches (15.2–20.3 cm) into the ground. It takes about ten minutes to stroll from the beginning to the center, which is set in a clump of trees. From time to time, Mills adds other elements to keep things interesting. "There's a fence on one side where I once put a stained-glass window that cast colors across the labyrinth. At one point, I had an old salon chair from the 1950s at the center of the labyrinth. Now there's a stone seat to sit on. Originally, I had a 30-foot (9 m) ladder that went up straight up in the air, and the idea was that once you had reached the center, you'd just keep going—metaphorically, anyway."

PART TWO:
STONEWORK
PROJECTS

The steel, slate, and buff tones of a bluestone
patio and stone retaining walls provide a soft contrast
to the pool-table green lawn and cerulean blue waters.

Chapter 6

STONE
ON YOUR OWN

THERE ARE MANY WAYS to bring stone into the home landscape through simple, straightforward, do-it-yourself projects. Precut stones make it easier to set a patio or walkway. Naturally squared rocks simplify erecting a wall. Prefab kits provide almost everything you need to build a small pond. But, when working with rocks and stones, caution is required, or what should be an enjoyable weekend project could result in anything from a bruised toe to a neighborhood power outage.

Beginners can find many resources, including how-to books, explanatory websites, and information from the local garden center or stone quarry. In addition to doing plenty of background research, you should also do field research, looking around at stonework installations in public

A group of mailboxes moves from functional to whimsical with a mosaic of stones set to make them appear as a tidy row of cottages.

These stones are set into a hillside to create what appears to be a naturally occurring, completely southwestern walkway and rock garden, with fire-red blossoms and the dramatic forms of aloes and cacti in many sizes.

gardens or your friends' backyards. Talk to people who have already embarked on a stone project; find out what they learned and what they might do differently if they had it to do over.

Think hard about not just what you need now but also what you'll need down the road. Is that intimate patio under the lilac bushes going to be a peaceful refuge for you and your spouse—or overrun when your family expands? Once you've installed that beautiful pond, will you really have the time to maintain it properly, or would a birdbath and fountain be a better choice for a water feature?

And when you've decided what it is you want and need, sketch it on paper and on site. Take proper measurements of the entire area to ensure you get the scale of your project right, and then use a hose, length of rope, or limestone dust to mark where you think you want the patio, pond, or walkway to be. Walk around, consider all the angles, and see if there's a better path or placement.

STARTING SMALL

It's probably a good idea to start with a small project first. Not only is working with rocks a tiring experience, but you can practice your skills and get a feel for the stone, as well as the materials and equipment required, by building a decorative planter near the back door before moving on to that 30-foot (9 m) stone wall you've been imagining; or set a few stepping stones before you decide to install a series of interconnected walkways.

Finally, be sure to put adequate time into the preparation of your site, for this is the most critical—and most frequently overlooked—step to ensuring overall success of the project. Create proper footings, foundation, gravel base, or whatever is appropriate to your project, and

you'll reduce maintenance requirements down the road. Because stones are heavy, you'll want to set them once and then leave them where they're supposed to be. You don't want to go back, lift, remove, and re-create a proper base when you discover a big puddle on your patio—or worse, in your basement—because the grade wasn't sloped adequately away from the house.

When you do move stones, use durable gloves and good lifting techniques, and enlist the aid of a wheelbarrow, pry rod, rollers, or a strong neighborhood teenager looking to make a few bucks. Most important, before you put a shovel in the ground anywhere, be sure you know the location of all utility, sewer, and water lines. Be sure to dial 811, the "Call Before You Dig" hotline in the U.S., or contact your international one-call center location. You will protect the infrastructure and possibly save a life. Your town's emergency crews are *not* the people you want rushing over to your house on a sunny spring day you've set aside for working in the garden.

▼ ▶ Innumerable black and white blocks are required to create this stunning, high-contrast pattern on this South American plaza.

DIY:
DRY-LAID FREESTANDING OR RETAINING WALL

STONE WALLS ARE OFTEN used to mark a boundary, such as the edge of a field or the border of a garden; to enclose a space such as a dining area; to retain or terrace a slope or recontour the yard; or to create a raised area, which may then be used for a patio or garden beds. Aside from these practical applications, stone walls can also be used—as seen in these pages—as stand-alone landscape elements that either define and enhance space or become sculptural, artistic elements in their own right.

Before building your own wall, study stone walls in your neighborhood as well as in this and other books. Keep the following instructions in mind as you think about the choices each waller made to create a stable and beautiful structure. Understanding what other craftsmen have done will help you tremendously as you plan your own wall and start placing individual stones.

When building a dry stone wall, consider these basic elements of technique. Most important: Remember that the force of gravity acting on the stones themselves is what keeps a stone wall together. Therefore, good stone wallers place each and every stone so gravity is working *for* rather than against it. Other key points—explained on the pages that follow—are to establish proper drainage, use tie stones at regular intervals, slope the wall inward, and avoid aligning vertical joints. These simple steps ensure your stone wall will not only be beautiful but still standing for the next generation to enjoy.

1

STEP 1: CHOOSING STONE

You can choose among many types of stone; a visit to your local garden center or stone yard will give you lots of ideas. In general, choose a type of stone that is naturally square in shape. This will make building much easier and the stone wall stronger. You also want to find stone that comes in different shapes and sizes, as you will need certain stones to perform specific jobs. To calculate how much stone you will need, multiply its length and height by thickness to get the volume. The staff at your garden center or stone yard will be able to translate the volume to square yards or tonnage of stone required. Always get more stone than you think you'll need; that way, you'll have plenty of stones to choose from to create the form, function, and face you want once you get into the actual building.

STEP 2: **EXCAVATION**

Stone walls require a solid and well-draining foundation. While some wallers simply take away the top, soft soil and lay stones directly on the firm subsoil, most contractors excavate 8 to 12 inches (20.3–30.5 cm) down, tamp the subsoil firm, and then install several inches of crushed gravel to provide a firm footing and good drainage for the stones. If you are building a straight wall, set up stakes and strings to guide the work; if your wall will curve, lay a hose or ropes on the ground to give you a visual cue to its path, then mark the lines with crushed limestone or spray paint before excavating.

3

STEP 3: BUILDING THE WALL

When you look at an established stone wall, you'll generally see the stones were laid in courses, or layers. Take a closer look, and you'll also notice that stones of varying sizes regularly interrupt the vertical and horizontal seams. This bridging of seams is important to maintain the strength of the wall. Just as a stone is easier to break when you give it a seam by scoring it with a chisel, so a stone wall is easier to break down when it has long, straight seams spanning multiple courses.

It's also important to ensure that each and every stone you lay is level and stable; wobbles will only get worse as you build upward. Use a carpenter's level to check placement, especially of your larger stones, and use small rock pieces to shim the edges of stones to create a level and solid placement. If you want to shape stone, score it with a chisel or brick set, set the stone over a lip with the part to be cut away hanging over the edge, and then hit the overhang with a small sledgehammer. But in general, try to use stones as you find them. It saves time and makes for a more natural-looking wall.

When you lay your first course, don't make the beginner's mistake of using the biggest stones on the bottom; you'll want those to help stabilize the wall as you build upward. Use large, flat stones on the first course to make a solid bed for the rest of the wall. And because this first layer is often partially under grade, you can use your ugliest stones here. As you lay courses, start with the corners of the wall and work inward to give yourself a structure. Choose stones for the corners that have two good, square faces.

Then as you add each layer, follow these guidelines:

Two over one, one over two: Never lay stones of the same size directly on top of one another. Like a pile of books stacked too high, the stones will tip over. Instead, break vertical seams by laying the stones more like brickwork, two stones with one crossing the seams beneath and above. Your wall will not only be stronger but also more natural looking and pleasing to the eye.

Batter the wall backward: As a stone walls builds up, it must slant inward slightly, either back into the slope if it's a retaining wall or from both sides upward if it's a double-faced wall. This is known as battering the wall. If you're making a retaining wall, you can set each course about $^1\!/_2$ inch (1.3 cm) farther back from the edge of the course below; if it's a double-faced wall, it should slope inward about 15 degrees from vertical. To help guide your upward progress, you can create a batter gauge—a straight board, about 2 by 4 inches (3.8 × 8.9 cm), with an appropriately slanting edge tacked on—which you can place against the face of the wall as you build. Use a level to hold the straight edge of the batter gauge plumb.

Use tie stones and deadmen: Tie stones are large enough to run the full width of the wall and span two or more horizontal joints. Deadman or bond stones are used in retaining walls, and they run deeper than the width of the wall, stretching into the area being retained. Tie stones and deadmen are critical to creating a strong wall; they function as a kind of anchor for the stones around them. It's generally recommended that you use tie stones and/or deadmen about every 4–6 horizontal feet (1.2–1.8 m), or as often as is practical.

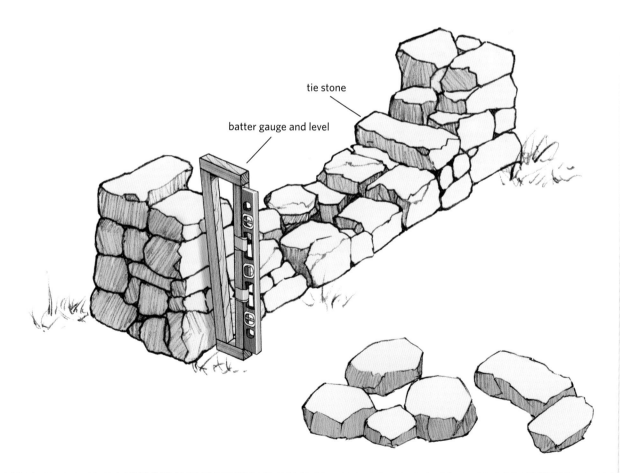

tie stone

batter gauge and level

Incorporate riser stones: Riser stones function like tie stones, only vertically. These tall stones create strength by bridging horizontal seams; they also give the wall visual interest and relief. Use riser stones to span two or more courses—again, about every 6 feet (2 m), or as frequently as is practical.

Set aside capstones: As you work, set aside broad, flat, substantial stones wide enough to span the wall. You can use these for the top of the wall to hold down the underlying stones and create a finished look.

Don't build too high: Dry stone walls should be no more than 3 to 4 feet (1–1.2 m) tall. Not only is it difficult to maneuver stones above this height, but anything taller may be unstable. Stone walls of this size also appear more natural in the home landscape.

Step back often: As you work, take time to step back from the wall to assess. Look for a balance and variety of stone sizes, clean lines, seams that have been bridged by tie and riser stones, and overall appearance. Taking a break not only gives your body a rest but also helps you see how the wall is shaping up and contributing to the landscape you're creating.

4

STEP 4: BACKFILL

If you're making a retaining wall, fill the area behind the wall nearly to the top with gravel to ensure good drainage and stability. When the wall is complete, top off the gravel fill just behind the wall with soil and sod or plantings, as appropriate to your site.

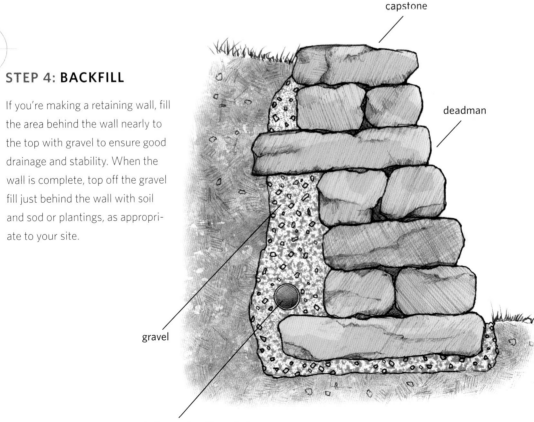

capstone

deadman

gravel

drainage pipe, if needed

TIPS

A Strong Back and a Careful Eye

- Check with your local utility companies to find all underground lines before you begin siting and excavating your wall. See page 112.

- Make sure each individual stone and each course of stones is level; stability problems will only increase as you build upward.

- Be cautious when lifting heavy stones. Use good lifting techniques and levers, rollers, ramps, or strong friends, neighbors, and family members to help as needed.

- Sort stones as you build, setting aside appropriately shaped stones to be used for risers, tie stones, and capstones.

- Get more stone than you think you'll need. This will give you plenty of stones to choose from so you'll always have the right stone to address both structural and aesthetic requirements. Excess stone can always be used for shims, back-fill, stepping stones, or decorative garden elements.

- If you're building a retaining wall, it's a good idea to consult with a professional, experienced landscaper first, even if you're going to do the work yourself. There are several important issues to consider. Creating proper drainage is one of the most important—to ensure all your hard labor will still be there for the coming generations to admire.

DIY:
DRY-LAID PATIO
OR WALKWAY

STONE MAKES AN EXCELLENT surface for walking, sitting, or entertaining areas. Not only is stone dry, flat, and available in many colors but it also offers an interesting counterpoint to green lawn and upright plantings; further, it makes a wonderful complement to other stonework, such as walls and ponds. Patios and walkways not only direct human traffic but also can work to tie an entire landscape together.

Choosing the right kind of stone is an important first step. While natural pieces of stone can create a lovely, rustic walkway or patio, keep in mind that the more random the stone shapes, the more challenging the patio will be to put together. Irregular surfaces will make for tippy chairs and table legs, so such stones are not the best choice if you're planning on a dining area or entertaining groups of people. Fortunately, many kinds of precut paving stones are readily available at garden centers and stone yards. The uniform thickness and square edges of these pavers make them easy to work with, even if you choose to use different shapes and sizes or create a randomized pattern. You can also consider combining different types of stone; however, unless you are very skilled, it's a good idea to keep the look and feel of materials fairly consistent. For example, use bricks or cobblestones with cut paving stones to keep a geometric consistency, or use the same kinds of stones, but select different color shades.

1

STEP 1: **SITE AND SIZE**

When planning where to put your patio or walkway, consider expected usage, traffic flow, and scale. Do you want a place where you and your spouse can sit quietly with a cup of coffee and the morning paper or a place to bring the whole family outside for a barbecue? Would you like to encourage visitors to walk to the side instead of the front door of the house? Or is there a special spot on the property you'd like people to discover, such as a pond or gazebo? Do you want a quiet little pathway for one through a shade garden, or a walkway large enough for a child's tricycle?

Once you have an idea of what you want the patio or walkway to accomplish, lay out the shape and size of the space using stakes and mason's string, spray paint, or even lines of flour. If you are creating a square or rectangular patio, be sure the dimensions are truly square by measuring all sides as well the diagonals; the width (A) and length (B) should measure the same on both sides, and the diagonal dimensions (C) should also be equal to one another. If you will be using informal stones and creating an organic shape, you can simply rough out the length and width you'd like the path or sitting area to be. Garden hoses are also handy for outlining a curving path or patio.

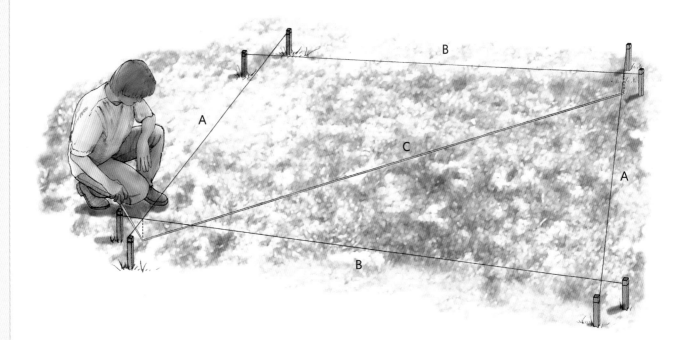

STEP 2: EXCAVATE TO CREATE AN APPROPRIATE SLOPE

Once the shape is established, excavate down far enough to accommodate the typical depth of stone you'll be using, plus a few inches more for a bed of sand in which to set the stones. For example, if you're using flagstones that are roughly 1 1/2 to 2 inches (3.8–5 cm) thick, you'll want to excavate about 4 to 5 inches (10.2–12.7 cm) down. Also, excavate a few inches beyond the perimeter of the patio or walkway to allow room to maneuver. Remove all sod and topsoil.

If you're building a patio, establishing a proper slope is critical to direct the flow of rain and runoff water. If the patio will be up against your home, pitch it away from the house's foundation. If you are building a freestanding patio, you can create a slope that moves in all directions away from the center. A walkway can follow the natural slope, as long as it's not pitched toward the foundation of your house or other building. It is suggested that patios have 1/8 inch (3 mm) of slope per foot (0.3 m) of stone, or 1 inch (2.5 cm) for every 8 feet (2.4 m). And if heavy flows or standing water and proper drainage are of real concern, you should excavate even more deeply and install several inches of crushed gravel as a base layer, underneath the sand bed. Many people feel a gravel bed should be installed no matter the circumstances, just to ensure stability and drainage. If you decide to use gravel (see illustration, page 132), you may want to install landscape fabric first. Also, be sure to compact it thoroughly before installing the sand bed, as noted on the following page.

Continually check the level of excavation as you go to establish proper grade. You may do this by setting up level lines (small levels that hang off lines strung between stakes) or by placing a carpenter's level on a long 2 by 4-inch (3.8 × 8.9 cm) board set on the ground in numerous directions and locations over the excavated area.

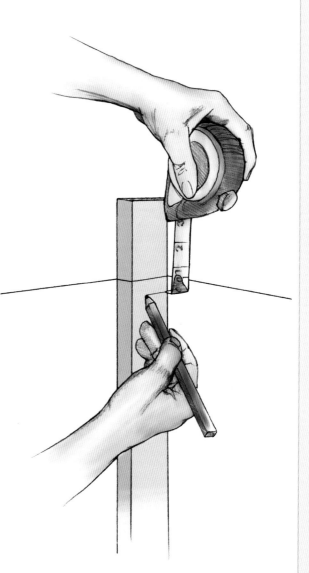

STEP 3: LAY A SAND BED

Once you have removed the topsoil, moisten and tamp the subsoil to compact it, and lay down landscape fabric over the entire area to deter weeds. At this stage, some people set up edging to hold the sand and, eventually, the stones. Many edging materials are available, from pressure-treated lumber to plastic or metal. In most cases, however, simply replacing and compacting the soil around the edges of the patio or walkway will hold the stones in place.

Once the patio or walkway location has been excavated, compacted, and covered with landscape fabric, fill the area with 2 to 3 inches (5–7.6 cm) of masonry sand (or with gravel first, then sand, as noted above, in areas with drainage problems). Smooth the sand with a rake and then reestablish a proper slope by pulling a long 2 by 4-inch (3.8 × 8.9 cm) screed across the sand. You may want to put up temporary forms to give your screed an appropriate level to run against. Moistening the sand with a fine mist can make it easier to smooth.

STEP 4: SET YOUR STONES

Begin in a corner and start to lay your stones. If you are using regular pavers, they will fit neatly together in a predetermined pattern. If you are using flagstones, you'll be putting together a make-your-own, somewhat abstract puzzle, looking for complementary shapes to fit one another. You can also cut stones yourself by scoring each side with a brick set or stone chisel, setting the stone over the edge of a piece of wood, and gently tapping off the excess edge with a small sledgehammer. Regardless of the stone material, make sure your joints are a consistent width. Tighter-fitting joints create a more formal appearance, while larger gaps achieve a naturalized, casual feel.

As you set each stone, shimmy it slightly to ensure a good setting in the sand. Check the level of each stone to ensure proper slope and elevation between the stones. If a stone is too high or wobbly, remove it and scrape away a layer of sand; if it's too low, add sand or stone chips underneath. When each stone is in place and leveled, tamp it into the sand with a rubber mallet.

CROSS SECTION OF WALKWAY CONSTRUCTION

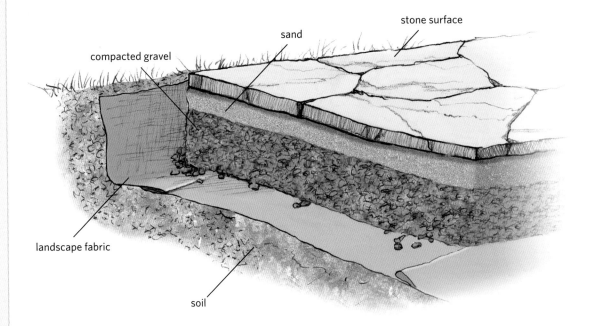

This cutaway view shows the various layers that will ensure a stable patio or walkway. After excavating, the soil layer must be compacted. Landscape fabric works to deter weed growth and holds the gravel above the soil. A few inches of compacted gravel improves drainage. A couple of inches of sand or rock dust creates an appropriate bed for settling stones or pavers. A final sweeping of sand or rock dust over the stones fills in cracks and keeps stones from shifting from side to side.

TIPS

Stability and Slope

- Check with your local utility companies to find all underground lines before you begin siting and excavating. (See page 112.)

- Make sure each individual stone is level.

- Be cautious lifting heavy stones. Use good lifting techniques and get help as needed.

- Over time, paving stones may settle or shift. Simply remove the stone, relevel the base, and replace the stone.

- Occasionally you will need to refill the joints of your patio with sand. You may also use rock dust between the stones in place of sand for a uniform color or use soil in the larger gaps and plant mosses, herbs, or other creeping plants between the stones.

- Mortared patios are a good option for a formal look or for heavily trafficked areas, places that require additional strength, such as along the edge of a pool, or where you want a completely weed-free environment. However, mortared patios and walkways are more difficult to build, require a concrete foundation, and crack over time, especially in cold climates, requiring repairs that are more difficult and expensive than simply resetting a stone here and there.

5

STEP 5: THE FINISHING TOUCH

Once all the stones are set, dump more sand onto the patio or walkway and use a broom to sweep it into the spaces between the stones. Water the patio to settle the sand, and repeat the process. (Some people use rock dust in a color complementary to the stonework instead of sand for this last fill-in-the-cracks stage.) Replace soil and sod along the perimeter of the space. If you have used natural stones with large gaps between them, you may want to fill in the gaps with topsoil instead of sand and plant creeping herbs or ground cover to grow along the gaps and soften the edges of the stones.

When *Not* to DIY:
Thoughts on Working with a Contractor

Few satisfactions are more complete than standing back from a complicated job and saying, "Wow, I did that myself." Conversely, few frustrations are more multifaceted than having a project take longer and cost more than you thought. For this and many other reasons, you may want consider using a contractor on a stonework job.

• **Cost:** While it seems that you'll save money doing the job yourself, the numbers don't always add up that way. Contractors pay less for materials, own or can easily rent equipment as needed, and are more experienced and faster than the average homeowner. There's also the value of your own time to consider, and the value a professionally installed project would add to your home. Sometimes paying a contractor is better for the bottom line.

• **Time:** There is also the problem of having a certain part of your home or yard out of commission while you put weekend number six into a project that was supposed to take a single Saturday afternoon—not to mention all the time you could be spending on other recreational activities or more manageable projects. Contractors have an incentive to finish the job well and quickly; they want to get on to the next job.

• **Expertise:** If you're doing a job for the first time, it's hard to anticipate everything that can go wrong. Contractors should know how to maximize the impact and functionality of a project as well as anticipate potential problems. Maybe you're not thinking about the maintenance a pond will take or that there's another easier way to get a water feature in the backyard. Have you considered the drainage implications of having a patio in the lower part of your yard? In a more positive vein, what about adding landscape lighting to make the yard come alive at night? Maybe if you include a wall alongside the walkway, you'll get some extra privacy, and as you're excavating anyway.... An experienced contractor can and should consider all such angles, alternatives, implications, and opportunities, and have the vision to design the project as well as the skill to install it beautifully.

• **Physical wear and tear:** Stones are heavy and hard. Drop one on your toe, and you could be headed to the hospital for a splint instead of to the fridge for a refreshing drink. Strain your back lifting and placing that stone, and you could be in bed for a week. Bringing in a contractor lets you leave the heavy lifting to the young bucks—and the expensive machinery.

Bruce Zaretsky's Advice for Working with a Pro

"Most homeowners are relying on guys like me as an expert, but many people in this industry are not experts and can get themselves in binds. If a contractor presents a really cool idea, it can be exciting, but you have to ask questions."

—B.Z.

The team at Zaretsky & Associates shows how it's done at this property in Victor, New York.

An existing deck was incongruous with the home's architecture and limited access to the yard.

The deck was torn down and the site cleared. Landscape fabric was placed to deter weeds and hold the gravel in place.

- Questions are important. Does it work in our climate? Have you done it before or seen it done before? What are the maintenance issues? Will you help me down the road if something goes wrong? Who will actually be doing the physical work on this project?
- Communication is critical. Even if the contractor seems great, check references, make sure they're insured, and think carefully about what it is you're asking of them. Homeowners should demand complete honesty and tell the contractor they want no surprises—or only happy surprises! Projects have the potential to end badly if one or both sides is holding back information. If either has any concerns, they should stop the job immediately and call an on-site meeting.

A semicircular retaining wall will hold a patio and create a gracious transition between house and yard. Each stone is leveled as it is placed, while stakes and strings are used to ensure proper height and grade.

A set of low steps between the house and patio creates a terraced effect, enhancing the sense of moving from interior to exterior spaces.

• Things can go wrong. Adversity shows the character of the person doing the work. You need to sit down and work through what went wrong, what happened.

• To keep costs to a dull roar, work with off-the-shelf materials. There's no need to bring in a metalworker to do a $15,000 (£7500) gate. You can do cool stuff with readily available materials and local craftspeople. An urn with water spilling out of it is a million-dollar effect for $300 to $1,500 (£150 to £750) Work within a 20-mile (32 km) radius to minimize travel time. Find an efficient team. Come up with cool ideas that don't cost a lot of money. *That*'s creativity.

Zaretsky & Associates is a landscape design, build, and consulting company near Rochester, New York.

Bluestone pavers are dry laid to create a patio. The pattern of the stones is continued to the edge, where the stones will be trimmed to fit.

Lights are installed in the stair risers. This not only enhances safety but also draws people out to the deck after dark and creates a beautiful glow on the stonework.

The finished project features an alternate pattern of pavers in the center of the patio for visual interest and to break up the large field of bluestone.

DIY:
GARDEN POND
WITH STONE SURROUND

A POND WITH A WATERFALL brings the soothing sight and sound of water over rocks to your landscape. Plus, it provides the opportunity to add aquatic wildlife and a marvelous group of plants to the garden setting.

Building a pond can be a straightforward proposition, especially if you purchase a complete kit, available at many garden centers or online sources. Even if you choose to make your water feature more customized or elaborate, the basic principles are the same. Backyard ponds are essentially holes lined with special rubber material, filled with water, and edged with sod and/or stones. Many people also line the inside of their ponds with stones and gravel both to protect the liner from ultraviolet (UV) exposure and to help create a more natural environment for beneficial bacteria and other aquatic life. A pump and filter system is vital to keeping the water moving, aerated, and clean.

GARDEN POND WITH STONE SURROUND

1

STEP 1: CHOOSING A SITE AND SHAPE

When selecting a site for your pond, consider where it will be viewed from: places your family gathers or entertains, such as the patio or deck, or living room windows, or the kitchen sink. Plan around the other landscape elements. For example, while a wooded area makes a lovely backdrop, if you place the pond too close to trees, you'll find their roots will interfere with digging, and their dropping leaves will create an ongoing cleaning challenge. Make sure the pond is close enough to your home that you can wander over with a cup of coffee or glass of wine, but not so close that it interferes with the natural flow of people and activities.

Once you have a site in mind, check with local utilities to identify the placement of underground lines. When you're sure you won't inadvertently cut into an electrical or sewer line with your shovel, use a rope or hose to lay out a natural-looking silhouette on the ground. Asymmetrical kidney shapes are pleasing and allow for multiple vantage points to enjoy the pond. Typically, backyard ponds are about 11 by 16 feet (3.4 × 5 m), but choose a size in balance with your yard and other landscape features. When the site and shape are determined, use spray paint, a hose, or crushed limestone to mark the outline.

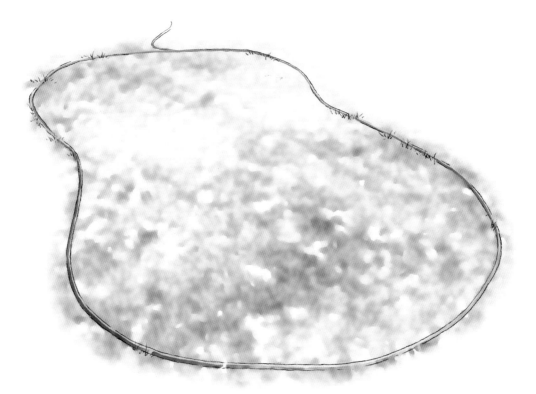

2

STEP 2: EXCAVATION

Now the hard work of digging begins. Most ponds include a ledge on which to place plants so they are at their preferred depth. This divides the pond into two shorter walls—a more stable design than a single tall one. Dig from the center outward, leaving a shelf 9 to 12 inches (23–30.5 cm) wide and 9 to 12 inches (23–30.5 cm) from the top. The overall pond depth can be anywhere from 14 to 24 inches (36 to 61 cm) deep, with gently sloping sides. Some also suggest sloping the bottom of the pond to create a shallow end that will facilitate draining and cleaning. Finally, dig a pit about 10 inches (25 cm) deep, and slightly larger in diameter than the pump, in the center of the pond; this is the pump pit.

It is critical that the top edges of the pond are level all the way around so water will not pour out on one side, exposing the other. Place a carpenter's level on top of a long 2 by 4-inch (3.8 × 8.9 cm) board all the way across the pond, and then add or take away soil from the rim as needed to ensure a level edge.

Pile excavated dirt into the area you have determined the waterfall will go. In most cases, the amount of excavated dirt makes a waterfall rise that is nicely proportioned with the size of the pond.

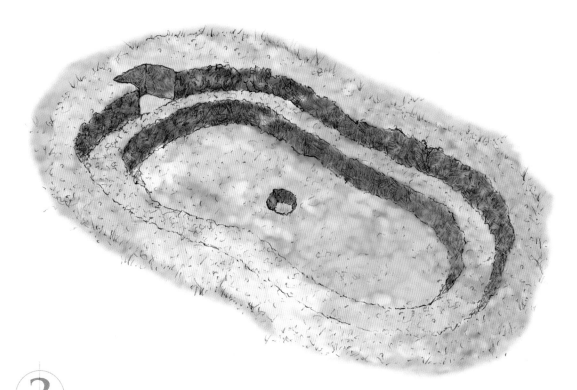

③ STEP 3: **BUILDING THE WATERFALL**

To create a waterfall, you want to build a natural-looking rise. Think of the waterfall as a kind of trough, and be sure to build up the edges to contain the water as it cascades down the falls. Create a terrace (or two), and make a shallow cavity behind the terrace to place the weir which catches water and acts as a reserve for the fall. As you build up the waterfall, be sure to tamp down the fill on a regular basis—every couple of inches—so the dirt won't settle in the future and dislodge rocks. You will also need to make a basin at the top of the falls to hold a weir or a skimmer that will act as a water reservoir.

STEP 4: LINING THE POND

Remove all rocks, roots, and other sharp objects from inside of the pond. Then, spread an inch or so (2.5 cm) of sand along the bottom of the pond and the ledge to create a protective layer for the underlayment and liner. Center a sheet of geotextile underlayment in the pond making sure you have a single piece big enough to extend well over the pond edges. Then, being careful not to drag it over any rough ground, place the folded rubber liner into the pond, unfold it so it overlaps equally on all sides, and then gently and loosely push it into the contours of the pond. Don't worry about fitting it exactly; the weight of the water will help hold the rubber liner against the walls of the pond. Spread the liner over the waterfall area. If you are using a separate liner from the one in the pond, make sure the two pieces overlap by at least 12 inches (30.5 cm) so water will not get under or between them.

5

STEP 5: SETTING THE STONES

Place stones horizontally against the vertical sides of the pond walls, overlapping them and using smaller stones to fill gaps. Lay flat stones along the pond bottom and ledge. You may also use gravel or river rock to fill in and create a natural look. Place a large, flat stone in the pump pit in the center of the pond, and run the pump hose from the pit up to the waterfall weir. Use stones to gently hold the hose in place.

Place a large, flat stone on each waterfall terrace, making sure it is level from side to side but tipped slightly forward and sticking out so it creates a lip for water to spill from. Attach the liner to the weir, and then place stones under the spillway, over the weir, and along the sloping sides and back of the waterfall. Take your time, stand back, and check your work often to ensure you're creating a natural-looking setting, with a balance of securely placed large and small stones or boulders.

Trim the liner to about 12 inches (30.5 cm) from the edge of the pond and waterfall. Then place large, flat coping stones along the perimeter of the pond (or bring sod up to the edges) and set the final stones around the edges of the waterfall. Give your waterfall a test run to make sure the water is going in the direction you intend. Then, as a final step, apply a thin bead of black waterproof foam sealant under and around the stones in the waterfall. This will not only help hold them in place but also will ensure the water goes over rather than under them.

6

STEP 6: **FILLING THE POND**

Before installing the pump, run a garden hose over all the stones in the pond and waterfall. Once the dirty water has collected, use a sump pump to remove it from the pond bottom. Then, place the pond pump on the flat stone in the center of the pond, and connect the hose between the pump and the weir. Carefully conceal the power cord for the pump through gaps in the stones and connect it to an appropriate weatherproof outlet. You should work with an electrician to ensure safe, all-weather installation of your pump and power source.

Now it's time to fill your pond with a garden hose; this may take several hours for a large pond.

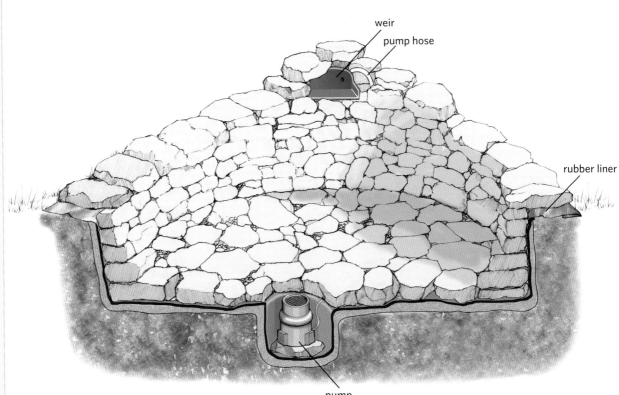

weir

pump hose

rubber liner

pump

Once the pond is full, you can start your pump and enjoy the visual and aural treat of water gently trickling over stones. Don't be concerned if your pond is cloudy at first; the dirt will settle and the water will clear within a few days. Let your pond rest for a couple of weeks so the water chemistry can stabilize; then add plants and fish as appropriate and desired.

TIPS

Preparation and Patience

• Check with your local utility companies to find all underground lines before you begin siting and excavating your pond. (See page 112.)

• Make sure the top edges of your pond are absolutely level so water doesn't drain out of one and expose the other.

• It may take two people to maneuver the pond liner. Don't leave it on the lawn in the sun, as it will heat up and kill grass; however, leaving it to warm up on a driveway or patio may make it more manageable.

• Use a combination of stones, boulders, gravel, and river rock inside your pond to create a natural setting for plants, fish, and beneficial bacteria; this will make your pond environment healthy and reduce maintenance needs.

• Let the water in your pond cure for at least two weeks before adding fish.

OUTDOOR STONEWORK

DIY:
ROCK GARDEN, STEPS, AND CAIRNS

OUTDOOR STONEWORK TAKES MANY FORMS for many reasons. As much as we may love the bursting blooms in a traditional, lush, perennial border, more subtle—perhaps even more sophisticated—pleasures may be had with a view of plants cascading around, over, and through rocks. Stone stairs can make a sloping area more accessible and safer, or provide a path through a gently rising garden landscape. Stones imply permanence, even in passing, as any regular hiker has seen stones set out to mark trail direction, the highest point of a mountain, or simply to note that someone has gone before. On the following pages, discover how to bring a rock garden, stone steps, or a cairn into your world.

ROCK GARDENS: PLANTS AND STONES

IF YOU ARE FORTUNATE ENOUGH to have a stony outcropping on your property, creating a rock garden can be as simple as filling in the small divots and depressions among the exposed stones and ledge with a firm, well-draining soil mix and placing appropriate plants in the pockets you have made.

If you want to create a rock garden from scratch, you must consider your site carefully. Generally, a sloping hill that gets plenty of sun is the most likely candidate, as rock garden plants tend to value heat, light, and good drainage. You may also place your rock garden in a shady area, but this will limit your choice of plants to mosses, ferns, hostas, and other woodland plants. As you look at the site, imagine how it might appear if it were naturally rocky.

Then, remove the sod and place stones of various sizes and shapes in clusters throughout the site by excavating holes large enough that you can set the stones securely into the hillside or ground. Leave open areas of differing sizes to accommodate a variety of plants.

Once the rocks are placed, it's time to choose the plants. Because rock gardens are somewhat harsh environments—and traditionally low maintenance—make sure you choose plants that don't require a lot of water or rich soil (unless, as mentioned previously, you are placing your garden in a shady area). Dwarf conifers, heaths and heathers, creeping herbs, sedums, and lavenders are all good choices for a sunny, stony garden. Check with the staff at your local garden center for advice and suggestions on which plants will thrive in the conditions you've created (or exploited) so you can have an ongoing series of changing blooms and color throughout the season.

If you are building a stone wall, another option is to place plants among the rocks as you build. Choose plants that favor extremely well-drained soil, such as herbs, sedums, and other drought-tolerant plants. Find a niche between stones, pack it with soil, spread the root mass of the plant into the gap, and poke more soil among the roots. A chopstick is an excellent low-tech tool for this task. If you are building a retaining wall, you can add plants as you go; use soil in a few places instead of gravel for filling in just behind the wall stones, place the stem of a plant among a gap in the rocks, and leave the growing top part to cascade down the rock face.

TIPS

Look Before You Lay Stone

- Because there are so many different ways to set up steps, rock gardens, and other stonework for the garden, it's a good idea to visit friends' yards, public gardens, and horticulture centers, and to look in books and online to collect ideas and inspirations.

- Before you actually set any stones, place a few here and there to get an overall sense of scale and flow. Seeing stones on site may change your ideas about what will work best. Where you once thought you'd run steps straight up a hill, you may find that you'd prefer a more meandering path. The rock that looks huge in the back seat of your car may seem quite small when set in that sunny spot where you're planning a rock garden.

- Choose plants carefully when you're putting them near your stonework. Stones are heat sinks that create dry and toasty conditions which will cause some plants, like creeping thyme, to spread all over, and will simply kill others. Your local garden center should be able to advise you on the most appropriate plant choices.

- Consider traffic flow and people pacing. A set of wide steps will encourage people to move more slowly, while curves will entice them to pause and consider the views. A cairn becomes an attractive landmark, which can lead people to an isolated part of the garden. And because there are plenty of plants that can tolerate being stepped upon from time to time, there's no reason not to tuck low-growing, sweet-smelling plants among the gaps in your patio, walkway, steps, or rock wall.

STEPS: ONE AT A TIME

BUILDING STEPS CAN BE thought of as building a series of small walls topped by miniature rectangular patios. In general, figure that your riser—the mini-wall portion of the stairs—should be 6 to 8 inches (15.2–20.3 cm) tall. The treads should be at least 12 inches (30.5 cm) deep, but you can create a different effect by having much larger treads or landings that encourage meandering and pausing to enjoy the surrounding views. You can also create a series of smaller steps interrupted by larger landings for variety.

To calculate how many steps you'll need, follow this formula: Divide the total rise (vertical distance) by the number of steps to get the height of each riser (including tread); divide the total run (horizontal distance) by number of steps to get the tread depth for each step (not accounting for tread overhang beyond the riser). Steps should be at least 36 inches (91.4 cm)-wide (or long from side to side); treads should be at least 10 inches (25.4 cm) deep; risers (step height) should be no more than 7 ¾ inches (19.7 cm); all risers should be equal to within ⅜" (1 cm). Artistic license can, of course, be taken to change pacing or reflect varying terrain.

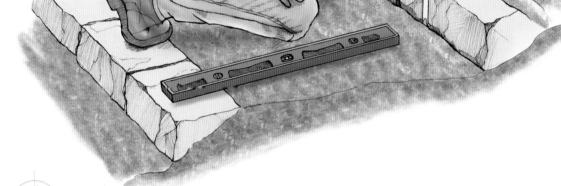

1 STEP 1: BUILDING THE RISERS AND SETTING THE TREAD

To begin, build the first two risers. Start at the bottom of the slope and excavate several inches into the soil. Because your riser will not be very high, you can generally find one or two stones that can be buried a few inches into the ground for stability and extend 6 to 8 inches (15.2–20.3 cm) above grade (at the front of the riser) to support the tread. If you are using more than one stone for the riser, make sure each is level with the other along the top so the tread will lie evenly across them. Next, excavate back into the slope so the ground is level with this first riser, as deep as you'd like your tread to go, and then set the next riser in the same way as the first.

Now it's time to set your tread. If you're using more than one stone, use the largest for the front part of the tread or landing, where most people will take their first step, as it must support the most force and weight. The larger the stone, the more stable it will be. You may want this front stone to overhang the riser just slightly for a more natural appearance. Then fill in around it with smaller stones. The same basic rules for patio building apply when you're creating treads. As you set each stone in the excavated area, ensure it is level but sloped just slightly forward to facilitate drainage, and that it is stable underfoot. Use sand, gravel, or rock dust to create a base and prop up stones or parts of stones that sit too low. Excavate where necessary to either lower stones that sit too high or create pockets to accommodate the uneven bottom surface of your rocks.

2

STEP 2: THE FINISHING TOUCHES

To finish your stairs, simply repeat the process
until you get to the top of the slope. The final
step is to fill in the cracks between and the areas
alongside the stones. Unlike on the patio, sand is
not the best filler for steps because the slope will
allow it to wash away. Instead, use compacted
rock dust or soil between and around the rocks.
Also, build up soil along the edges of the stairway
to hold the steps into the slope. Fill in the cracks
with creeping ground cover, if you wish, and
replace sod or install gardens along either side
of the stairs.

CAIRNS: LEAVING YOUR MARK

SOMETIMES CAIRNS ARE MORE FORMAL affairs, with plaques embedded in the stone; sometimes a bottle with notes to other travelers is left among the rocks. As human traffic has increased in wild places, the building of cairns has actually become somewhat controversial. Environmentalists fear that removing stones from footpaths and surrounding areas may increase erosion, damage delicate mountain ecosystems, or simply violate the leave-no-trace ethic. Others feel there is an inherent egotism in leaving a mark that essentially says to other hikers, "I was here first," and mars the sanctity of wild places.

So, if you'd like to build a cairn, it's probably a good idea to restrict your efforts to private property. Be sure to get permission from the landowner if you're building anywhere other than on your own land. The simplest cairns are groups of rocks, collected right on site, piled loosely but with the obvious intervention of human hands. If you'd like a more ambitious cairn, follow the basic building techniques outlined in the chapter on stone walls, but instead of building lengthwise, build up into a kind of teepee shape. Start with large, flat stones laid in a circular base. As you build each course, make the circumference of the circle a bit smaller, so the shape narrows as it goes up. You may also decide to use stones placed on edge rather than flat so they lock together in intersecting rows that spiral upward. If you plan to build an especially tall cairn, you will need equipment to lift you to the top. A ladder will keep you too far away from the peak, but if you have or know someone with a tractor, you can stand in the bucket of the front loader and get lifted—along with your stones—to appropriate building height. An even better—and far safer—idea is simply to keep your cairn at human height.

RESOURCES

811

National call-before-you-dig number, which should always be used to protect vital energy and telecommunications infrastructure.

About Stone

www.aboutstone.org

An international, non-commercial information resource for people who work with natural stone, including links, a discussion group, and a directory of stone sculptures.

The American Society of Landscape Architects

www.asla.org

National professional association of landscape architects, including listings and information about affiliated landscape architects across the country.

Bob Vila

www.bobvila.com

Official Bob Vila home improvement site, with a how-to library including step-by-step photos and instructions on building a stone wall and other stone, brick, and around-the-home projects.

The Botanic Gardens Trust of Sydney, Australia

www.rbgsyd.nsw.gov.au

Dedicated to inspiring the appreciation and conversation of plants; includes information about the Royal Botanic, Mount Annan, and Mount Tomah Gardens in Sydney, Australia.

Dig Safe

Most states have a web site and toll-free number to call to ensure protection of power, sewer, and communications lines. An online search will quickly locate this critical information that helps protect infrastructure and saves lives.

DIY Network

www.diynetwork.com

Tips and advice for a wide variety of do-it-yourself projects inside and outside the home, including building a stone fire pit.

Do It Yourself or Not

www.diyornot.com

Interactive application that compares professional versus do-it-yourself costs for a variety of projects, including laying a stone patio.

Dry Stone Wall Association of Australia

www.dswaa.org.au

Fosters the preservation and contemporary interpretation of Australia's dry stone walls and structures and advocates for preservation and the craft of walling.

Dry Stone Wall Association of Canada

www.dswac.ca

Membership includes a large cross section of people interested in dry stone walling techniques, as well as dry stone wall preservation. Offers demonstrations and education.

Dry Stone Walling Association of Great Britain

www.dswa.org.uk

An organization committed to the preservation of dry stone walls throughout Great Britain and to training people in the craft of dry stone walling, also known as drystone dyking.

Dry Stone Conservancy

www.drystone.org

Focuses on preservation of historic drystone structures, advancing the drystone masonry craft, and creating a center for training and expertise nationwide.

Extreme How-To

www.extremehowto.com

The "Enthusiast's Guide to Home Improvement" includes articles from the magazine and instructions for many around-the-house projects, including those in stone.

HGTV

www.hgtv.com

Ideas, inspirations, plans, and how-tos for the home and garden, from the television shows.

The Stone Foundation

www.stonefoundation.org

A society of stonemasons and others involved with or interested in stone, stonework, and stone art, including professional and amateur artisans, artists, architects, designers, suppliers, carvers, and others.

The Stone Wall Initiative

www.stonewall.uconn.edu

A regional coalition of stone wall enthusiasts, including educators, conservationists, and outdoor professionals, promoting the appreciation, investigation, and conservation of stone walls in New England.

ARCHITECTS AND DESIGNERS

Craig Bergmann Landscape Design
Wilmette, Illinois
www.craigbergmann.com

biota, A Landscape Design + Build Firm
Steve Modrow
Jim Saybolt
Minneapolis, Minnesota
www.biotalandscapes.com

Krugel Cobbles
Lake Bluff, Illinois
www.krugel.com

John and Rose Dejardin
Wingwell Garden
Wing, Rutland County, England

**The Botanic Gardens Trust of
    Sydney, Australia**
Geoff Duggan
New South Wales, Australia
www.rbgsyd.nsw.gov.au

**Hursthouse Landscape Architects &
    Contractors**
Robert Hursthouse
Bolingbrook, Illinois
www.hursthouse.com

Douglas Hoerr Landscape Architecture
Chicago, Illinois
www.douglashoerr.com

Michael Glassman & Associates
Michael Glassman
Sacramento, California
www.michaelglassman.com

Land Expressions LLC
Kathy Swehla
Mead, Washington
www.landexpressions.com

Ken Mills
Burlington, Vermont

Andrea Morgante
Hinesburg, Vermont

Clive Nichols
Chacombe, Banbury, Oxom, England
www.clivenichols.com

**Rocco Fiore & Sons, Inc.,
    Landscape Architects**
Drew Johnson
Libertyville, Illinois
www.roccofiore.com

Dry Stone Wall Association of Canada
John Shaw-Rimmington
Ontario, Canada
www.dswac.ca

Schmechtig Landscape Company
Mundelein, Illinois
www.schmechtiglandscapes.com

New Directions in Landscape Architecture
Greg Trutza
Phoenix, Arizona
www.gregtrutza.com

Terragram Landscape Architecture
Vladimir Sitta
New South Wales, Australia

H. Keith Wagner Partnership
Keith Wagner
Burlington, Vermont
www.hkw-p.com

Samuel H. Williamson & Associates
Sam Williamson
Portland, Oregon
www.shwa.net

Landworks Design
George Workman
Newcastle, Maine

Zaretsky and Associates, Inc.
Bruce Zaretsky
Macedon, New York
www.zaretskyassociates.com

PHOTOGRAPHER CREDITS

Carolyn Bates/www.carolynbates.com, (11, middle, left); 16–17; 18–19; 21; 23; 28; 29; 30; 31; 107

Courtesy of biota, A Landscape Design + Build Firm, 66; 67; 68; 69

Linda Oyama Bryan/ Schmechtig Landscape Company, 101

Linda Oyama Bryan/Craig Bergmann Landscape Design, 5

Linda Oyama Bryan/Rocco Fiore & Sons, Inc., Landscape Architects, 46; 47; 48

Linda Oyama Bryan/Krugel Cobbles, 53

Linda Oyama Bryan/Douglas Hoerr Landscape Architecture, 38; 39; 40; 41

Geoff Duggan/Mount Annan Botanic Garden, 11 (right); 105; 106

Courtesy of Rocco Fiore & Sons, Inc., Landscape Architects, 49

Amy Gallo Photography, 6 (middle); 50; 51; 52

Tria Giovan/www.triagiovan.com, 6 (left); 122; 146

Hausman Photography, 42; 43; 45

Dency Kane/www.dencykane.com, 7 (middle); 136

Douglas Keister/www.keisterphoto.com, 110; 111; 112; 113

Hans Matschukat, 3; 77; 74; 74; 75; 76; 77; 78; 109 (middle, left)

Clive Nichols Garden Photography/www.clivenichols.com, 12; 20; 55 (left); 79 (middle); 82; 83; 84; 85; 86; 87; 96; 97; 98; 99; 100

Norm Plate/New Directions in Landscape Architecture, 57; 58; 59; 60; 61

John Shaw-Rimmington, 6, (middle); 7 (right); 11 (left); 24; 25; 26; 27; 102; 103; 104; 154

Courtesy of Vladimir Sitta, Terragram Landscape Architecture, 54; 80 (right)

Brian Vanden Brink, 33 (left); 80 (left); 108

Brian Vanden Brink/Elliott Elliott Norelius Architects, 32

Brian Vanden Brink/Horiuchi & Solien Landscape Architects, 8; 9 (left & right); 10; 33 (right); 79 (bottom); 151

Brian Vanden Brink/Scott Simons Architects, 79 (top)

Brian Vanden Brink George S. Workman, Landscape Architect, 35

Courtesy of H. Keith Wagner Partnership, 22; 92; 93; 94; 95

Jessie Walker/www.jessiewalker.com, 14; 15; 55; 81; 114

Brian Westbury/Hursthouse Landscape Architects & Contractors, 62; 63; 64; 65; 109 (right)

Courtesy of Sam H. Williamson & Associates, 11 (middle, right); 70; 71; 72; 73; 88; 89; 90; 91; 109 (left)

George S. Workman, Landscape Architect, 34; 37

Bruce Zaretsky/Zaretsky and Associates, Inc., 109 (middle, right); 132; 133; 134; 135

Scot Zimmerman, 13

ACKNOWLEDGMENTS

Much appreciation is due the architects, designers, dry stone wallers, and homeowners who so generously shared their inspiration and callus-inducing work with me and, thereby, with our readers.

Many thanks to Winnie Prentiss, Laura Smith, Betsy Gammons, David Martinell, Phil Schmidt, and the rest of the Quarry team that made this book not only possible, but a pleasure to write.

As always, my deepest gratitude is reserved for JEL, without whom the best parts of my life and work would not be possible.

ABOUT
THE AUTHOR

Laurel Saville writes books, articles, essays, short stories, brand strategy, and corporate communications from her home in Albany, New York. She is also author of *Design Secrets: Furniture,* and the forthcoming book, *100 Habits of Successful Publication Designers,* © 2008, Rockport Publishers.

www.laurelsaville.com